Strategic Planning in a Rapidly Changing Environment

Strategic Planning in a Rapidly Changing Environment

James B. Whittaker
Georgetown University

Lexington Books
D.C. Heath and Company
Lexington, Massachusetts
Toronto

Library of Congress Cataloging in Publication Data

Whittaker, James B.
Strategic planning in a rapidly changing environment.

Includes index.
1. Corporate planning. 2. Southern California Edison Company
I. Title.
HD30.28.W45   658.4'01   77-4538
ISBN 0-669-01484-2

Copyright © 1978 by D.C. Heath and Company.

Published simultaneously in Canada.

Printed in the United States of America.

International Standard Book Number: 0-669-01484-2

Library of Congress Catalog Card Number: 77-4538

To my family

Contents

x

List of Tables

Preface

This book illustrates the concept of strategic planning for an audience of managers in complex organizations. These organizations may be business, nonprofit, large government, or other types of organizations. The reader will gain a better awareness of the complexity of strategic planning and how effective strategic planning requires a great deal of management effort to formulate corporate strategies and even greater management effort to effectively implement these strategies.

Part II describes in detail the application of strategic planning in a major United States firm and the environment of the energy industry in the United States from 1960 to 1975. Then a detailed description is given of the strategic planning process of Southern California Edison Company. Finally, the Southern California Edison Company's strategic planning process is evaluated using four different measurement standards.

Part III describes research findings of strategic planning, makes recommendations to management based on that research, and summarizes the concept of strategic planning.

**Strategic Planning in a
Rapidly Changing
Environment**

**Part I
The Concept of
Strategic Planning**

1 Introduction

Planning is one of the most fundamental activities of management. All managers plan and there are a myriad of types of planning and plans. Planning, as a concept, has been with us for a long time. Consequently, there are a variety of definitions for planning. However, in this book we are specifically interested in one type of planning—strategic planning. Strategic planning is concerned with both the definition of goals and objectives for an organization and the design of the functional policies, plans, and organizational structure and systems to achieve those objectives.

Why Strategic Planning?

Why should managers be interested in strategic planning? Managers exist in rapidly changing environments. In the past management was required not only to understand the environment in which the company existed but also to take action that would have some effect in setting the environment, thereby acting to the benefit of the organization. However, the changes occur much more rapidly today. As management interacts with rapidly changing economic, social, political, ecological, and technological environments, it is having difficulty understanding those environments, much less impacting them to the benefit of their respective organizations.

Consequently, it is necessary to approach this task in a new and different manner. Past planning techniques must be changed to enable management to effectively cope with rapidly changing environments. New methods must be developed to assist management in coping with the environmental threats and opportunities. Organizational structures must be analyzed in order to determine what changes are required for companies to be able to compete more effectively in their chosen markets.

Many times we sit back and plan too easily. We go through a process, establish a number of given conditions, determine the strengths and weaknesses of the organization, and develop a plan to resolve all the problems and set the optimum future course of action for the organization. However, the ease of accomplishment should be a caution light regarding the ultimate benefit to the organization. Experience has shown that often the easier the environmental analysis, the easier the corporate self-analysis, and the easier the integration of both these analyses into a reasonable plan

3

for the organization, the more suspect the result. Management must learn to deal with change that is more massive than ever before precisely because it exists in a more rapidly changing world. When planning is the most difficult and the results may be the most tenuous, we are dealing with the most uncertainty at a time when the firm has the greatest need for strategic planning. Planning is hardest when potential contributions are the greatest. When conditions are very stable with little change from year to year, the incremental value of planning is low. When an organization is involved in a changing, unstable environment, it is precisely these characteristics that require an organization to plan. The incremental value of strategic planning to corporate decision making will generally be much higher in the latter case.

What Is Strategic Planning?

But what about semantics? What do we mean by the term *strategic planning*? One way to differentiate management in a firm is to use the term *strategic management*, or *operational management*. Simply stated, strategic management encompasses those management actions that deal with the direction of the firm's resource allocation process. It relies heavily on a process called strategic planning. Strategic planning involves (1) analyzing the environment of the firm to determine specific threats and opportunities; (2) evaluating the firm to determine the key skills and resources that could be used to develop a competitive strategy in a given product-market situation; (3) integrating the unique skills and resources with the specific opportunities in the firm's environment; (4) establishing corporate objectives for where the company wants to be at a certain time; and (5) creating a number of corporate policies, plans, programs, and tasks to successfully accomplish the objectives that were established.

Strategic management, then, is one of the fundamental tasks of top management in an organization. Operational management, on the other hand, functions at lower levels to ensure that the strategy is carried out throughout the organization. The difference between strategic and operational management is important and should be kept in mind throughout this book. This is not to say that running a functional department efficiently is less important than deciding where the company should be in a given product market three years from now and developing corporate objectives and plans of action to make sure that occurs. It only means that in this book we are concerned with the concept of strategic management and how the concepts of strategic planning enable the firm to exist in an environment that changes more rapidly than in the past. Furthermore, there is no indication that the pace of change will slow; if anything, management must be *more* able to react to more change. The strategic planning function will be that much more difficult and consequently that much more important.

Drucker on Strategic Planning

Peter Drucker has made the interesting point that managers should know what strategic planning is *not*. It is not a box of tricks, a bundle of techniques; it is not forecasting. It deals not with future decisions but with the futurity of present decisions, and it is not an attempt to eliminate risk. These comments are helpful in understanding strategic planning. Too much effort has been expended in following initiatives in some of these areas to the long-run detriment of effective strategic planning.

Although there are certainly times where various analytical techniques must be used in strategic planning, they should be used as tools to accomplish the planning, not viewed as ends in themselves. Many firms are finding that increased use of the computer is necessary in strategic planning since it allows them to utilize a larger number of variables and consequently develop many more contingency plans than previously. Rigorous analysis must be used in the process of strategic planning, but simply quantifying everything one can lay one's hands on is not strategic planning.

The future will always be unpredictable and difficult to forecast. Consequently, we must plan strategically because we cannot forecast the future with certainty. Could the major automotive firms forecast that gasoline would be 60 cents a gallon in the mid-1970s? It has been said that this prediction was made in several of the major corporations but that the prediction had such a low probability that major decisions were not changed. It is always possible that certain future events may be anticipated by some. But the critical part of the analysis is whether that awareness will be sufficiently internalized in the major decision-making process that corporate behavior will be changed by the forecast. The future will probably be more, not less, difficult to forecast than in the past. Thus the importance of strategic planning will increase.

Finally, strategic planning enables us to choose rationally among risky endeavors. We are not attempting to eliminate or reduce risk. We do want to allocate resources to those endeavors having the appropriate return-risk profile consistent with the corporate objectives that we have established.

A Model for Strategic Planning

Consequently, Drucker calls strategic planning

a continuous process of making present entrepreneurial (risk-taking) decisions systematically and with the greatest knowledge of their futurity; organizing systematically the efforts needed to carry out these decisions; and measuring the results of these decisions against the expectations through organized, systematic feedback.[1]

This is an interesting definition because it provides a critical measure of a performance standard to use in the evaluation of strategic planning systems. It provides a useful construct by which a strategic planning system can be analyzed to determine whether these characteristics are found in the planning system of organizations. The first characteristic is that the system should be a continuous process. That automatically eliminates many "strategic planning" systems because they are spasmodic. It has been said that strategic planning is somewhat more of an art than a science and that this continuous-process criterion is thus somewhat irrelevant. There is some truth to that. Suffice it to say at this stage that this is not the only condition that must be found in order to have an effective strategic planning system.

Second, the process must be concerned with entrepreneurial or risk-taking decisions. Many decisions are made in organizations each day that are not risk-taking decisions. Many daily decisions are made to ensure that the operations of the firm continue. These decisions are not entrepreneurial and therefore are not in the subset of the firm's decisions involved with the strategic planning system. Third, the organization must be structured to implement the decisions reached in the strategic planning process. In many firms, the strategic planning process is laid on an existing organization and expected to achieve optimum results. This situation causes various organizational and efficiency problems. If the firm, in order to exist, must marshal its resources and compete in various product markets with its most effective corporate ability, then it follows that the organization must be restructured from time to time. Firms should not reorganize every time there is a slight shift in the environment. That would be counterproductive since it appears that managers know how to reorganize better than anything else. It simply means that the organizational structure must allow management to implement the strategic decisions of the organization.

Finally, the system must provide systematic feedback. When risk-taking decisions are made, there are certain expectations based on those decisions. The system fails if a systematic feedback mechanism is not installed. Decisions are made that have serious consequences on the long-run viability of the firm. The time frame of these decisions may be short or long term. However, no matter the term, the system must provide feedback to allow management to know whether reality is measuring up to expectations. The benefit of a strategic planning system is that the firm's decision makers can deal effectively with their environment. However, because of the uncertainty of the situation, continuous feedback on a periodic basis is needed to determine the firm's progress in the marketplace.

Increased Role of Strategic Planning

It is not difficult to understand why there is increasing emphasis on strategic planning and strategic management in today's very uncertain and rapidly changing world. Strategic planning will be more difficult in the future, but it is also more critical to the long-run efficacy of the firm. As the economy slows down and ever-increasing annual increments in sales are not ensured, the management of United States corporations will slowly change. Resources will be allocated with increasing caution as the environment becomes more uncertain. Firms will have to plan today, for tomorrow has never been more uncertain and that trend is unlikely to slow down. The stakes will be increasingly high as the corporate decision maker evaluates the various inputs of the decision process and consistently makes the "right" decision for the corporation. Strategic planning processes will provide more alternatives in the future, and so a greater variety of scenarios can be addressed. The use of computers to provide more alternative strategies will increase. Planning horizons will be extended as firms are forced to plan further into the future. Firms must be able to respond much more rapidly than in the past to short-term perturbations. Strategic planning alternatives will be developed for a variety of short-term outcomes in order to cope more fully with the rapidly changing environment.

Overview of the Book

The remainder of this book will take the reader through the various aspects of strategic planning. Topics to be covered include organizing for strategic planning, the business review, the environmental review, corporate assumptions, corporate objectives, developing alternate strategies, developing business policies and business plans, and implementation. Then an actual environment—the environment of the energy industry—will be depicted, and the strategic planning system of Southern California Edison will be described and then analyzed using several conceptual models. Finally, the implications of strategic planning for corporate management will be presented.

Note

1. Peter F. Drucker, *Management: Tasks, Responsibilities and Practice*, New York: Harper and Row, 1973, 1974, p. 125.

2 Organizing for Strategic Planning

Strategic planning may be accomplished in a firm in a variety of ways. These include, but are not limited to, (1) a committee process, (2) a separate staff function, (3) a line or business unit, (4) top executive management, (5) an outside consultant, (6) a task force, and (7) a combination of the above. The organization for strategic planning should be compatible with and support the objectives of the organization. Organizing for organization's sake is not the desired objective. The method of organizing is not nearly as important as whether the organization achieves an effective strategic planning process that allows it flexibility in its rapidly changing environment. Strategic planning is, to some extent, an art more than a science; so there may be more than one best way to organize, given the appropriate circumstances. However, we should look at the function of strategic planning and see where the responsibility for it resides. The top management of an organization is responsible for the strategic management of the firm. If the firm does poorly or fails, top management is responsible. The specific responsibility for strategic management resides with the chief executive officer. Given the right organization and the appropriate circumstances, any of the organizational methods cited could be used effectively. However, without the personal involvement in and commitment to the strategic planning process, none of these organizing methods will be effective. The chief executive officer is the critical component of an effective strategic planning system.

Committee

Strategic planning by a committee process involves the utilization of representatives from various line and staff units throughout the organization to accomplish the planning. Each member brings to the committee certain expertise representing the various parts of the organization. A committee chairman may be appointed by top management, but the responsibility for the planning rests with the total committee membership. Benefits from this approach include the unusual experience of the individuals assigned which allows the commmittee to more effectively resolve the issues before it. Since the committee will have broad organizational membership, a corporate view arises out of committee deliberations. One of the major

9

drawbacks of the committee approach is that, with such broad membership, there is no one corporate position responsible for the results of the strategic planning.

Separate Staff Function

Although it may be an attractive option that has worked in some instances, the establishment of a separate staff function to accomplish strategic planning has several major drawbacks. The most serious is that if the responsibility for strategic planning is left solely to the staff, line management will be cut out. It is difficult enough to get line management really involved in and dedicated to strategic planning. But if the total responsibility is given to a staff unit, even though it is staffed with very competent people and reports at a top management level, it will not produce the type of results the firm needs. The nature of strategic planning is such that it is involved with very uncertain areas. Difficult judgments must be made involving major allocations of scarce resources. Normally, staff units do not have the background and expertise to handle these difficult areas. More important, they will not have the responsibility of implementing the plan once it is approved. Even if the staff personnel have had recent experience in these areas, organization must deal with an increasing rate of change in their environments. During the past decade, many strategic planning staffs have been developed. This was a necessary first step as the process of strategic planning was developed. However, now that we know much more about strategic planning, there is a definite place for staff units to have coordination and assistance responsibilities, but it is inappropriate for them to do all strategic planning for the organization.

Line or Business Unit Management

Effective strategic planning should usually be accomplished by either line management or business unit management in large, diversified companies. The essence of strategic planning is to determine where the company wants to go in the future. To get there, certain analyses must be made of the company, its products, and its environment. All this information must be integrated into an effective plan for the firm. Line management must be involved in this process to ensure both that the assumptions upon which these plans are built are reasonable and that the plans can be executed. Line management must make sure that the plan is eventually carried out. Just as it is a strength to have line management accomplish the planning and then execute the plan, it is also a weakness to have a separate staff organization accomplish the planning and then expect line management to make it happen. If line management has the responsibility for developing the plan and then reporting results against that plan, the planning process will quickly get an infusion of credibility and realism that may have been lacking previously. There is no substitute for line management's accepting and supporting the planning process. Consequently, there are few methods of organizing that will approach the efficacy of having line management actually do the basic strategic planning for its organization.

Top Management

Another organizational alternative is to have strategic planning performed by top executive management. Strategic planning is a top management responsibility. However, generally they should not be the only ones to engage in it. An obvious exception to this statement is a small organization. In a small organization that has a small group of managers, probably the managers not only will be responsible for strategic planning but also will be the only group in the organization that has the capability to accomplish it. Strategic planning in a firm has little or no likelihood for success if it is not supported by and involved with the top management of the firm. These individuals have experience and daily contacts which are different from those of all other managers in the firm. Some crucial aspects of the firm's environment cannot really be fully understood or adequately analyzed unless the experience with and the understanding of those environments are communicated by the top executive management. Consequently, since strategic planning is a basic responsibility of top management and since the system will function much less efficiently, if at all, without the critical inputs of top management, the question is: Just what role should they play? In small firms, top management may do all strategic planning. As a firm grows, however, the main responsibility for the process must be passed on to another group of individuals. Top management should never set this new group off in a room and tell them to come back in 12 months with a strategic plan for the next year. The strategic planning function must have the personal involvement and support of top management. Consequently, top management should interact with this process no less often than monthly. Many companies have this interaction on a weekly basis. However, in this case, the strategic planning process must be well integrated with the firm's decision-making process. Being integrated means having an impact on the decisions made in the firm. Until the strategic planning process is so structured and so effective that major decisions in the firm are effected by the concept of strategic planning, the firm has a long way to go in its successful implementation of the process.

Outside Consultant

Strategic planning in a firm can be aided by an outside consultant. Initially, a consultant can advise on how to establish a strategic process. There are a variety of corporate planning firms and consulting organizations associated with public accounting firms that can advise an organization and actually establish a strategic planning organization within the firm. Some of these suggestions would be nothing more than a general fabric for a strategic planning process that would be especially tailored to the specific firm. There are benefits to be derived from receiving outside assistance from qualified personnel in this area since there are very few "organizational wheels" that have not been developed before. In addition, professional personnel who have seen a variety of systems can often provide very sound advice on experiences in similar situations. On the other hand, there is much to be said for the effectiveness that grows with a system that is developed in-house with competent people from the right organizational level. They know the business of the organization and can spend their time transferring this knowledge into an effective strategic planning system instead of educating outside consultants.

In addition to using outside consultants to initially introduce strategic planning, many times a firm will find it necessary to go to outside consultants to deal with a particularly difficult problem of environmental analysis. A firm may be entering a new field, or a major change may be developing in an environment that has never been particularly difficult. It may be wise to use professional assistance in this and similar cases in order to more adequately develop the strategic plan.

Task Force

Many organizations also use the task force approach. When a problem of strategic consequence arises, a task force will be assembled. Competent personnel from across the firm will be convened for a time to develop an effective strategy. After a specified time (it may be two weeks or six months), the task is accomplished and the personnel resume their previous responsibilities. The task force approach allows good people from all over the firm to be involved wherever necessary to accomplish the strategic planning.

Summary

There are a variety of organization alternatives for establishing a strategic planning process in an organization. No matter which alternative is chosen, it is a difficult process. In any but the smallest organization, the time frame to install an effective strategic planning system will run from three to five years. To effectively develop a strategic planning system, much coordination and analysis must be accomplished. The environment of the organization must be analyzed to determine the thrust and opportunities. A corporate self-analysis must be completed to determine the unique organizational capabilities in such areas as physical, financial, and personnel resources. Many decisions must be made, and plans need to be developed. All this must be accomplished in addition to the normal operating functions of the organization. Developing an effective strategic planning process in an organization will take three to five years. Many lessons will be learned and relearned over that period, but the development and maturation process takes time.

Strategic planning in organization is accomplished by a variety of methods. Depending on the type of system they are using, various organizations may use committees, task forces, or outside consultants. However, if top management is not involved, the system will not be effective. Strategic planning is a necessary endeavor for a successful firm. How the organization organizes for strategic planning and then implements the process is less important than the fact that the planning is accomplished.

3 Corporate Self-Analysis

One of the major foundations of effective strategic planning is the self-analysis a company must make to assess its past performance and its present position. Strategic planning built upon an unrealistic assessment of the strengths and weaknesses of the company will be of marginal value. Strategic planning is a process to allow the company to more effectively compete in a rapidly changing environment. If the assessment of the firm's past performance and present position is faulty, the entire process will miss the intended mark.

Analysis of Skills and Resources

The review of the firm must be thorough and realistic. Various alternative strategies will eventually be developed based on this very critical analysis. Companies are made up of a variety of skills and resources. They include human resources, financial resources, physical assets, and intangible resources. The objective of the self-analysis is to determine which of these skills and resources are unique. What capability does the firm have that is truly unique? What can this firm contribute to a market that other firms in the same market cannot?

Examples of Resources

The objective is quite clear. A number of firms in the United States are competing in markets where they have similar assets and skills but lack the unique capability that the leaders of the industry have. In a highly technical field, the unique skill or resource that is required to compete effectively is a particular group of engineers with a great deal of research experience and a long line of commercially successful products that they have developed. An example of an intangible resource might be goodwill that a company had earned in one field that was readily transferable to a product line or another commercial endeavor in another field. A unique resource might simply be a very strong financial position that a company would bring into an emerging industry that was formerly made up of many small, technically competent, but woefully underfinanced companies. Since the energy situation has changed so quickly in the past five years, many companies may have unique energy sources that can be used in periods when the rest of the industry is on reduced power allotments. It is hard to list even a small number of the unique skills or resources that a company could potentially have. The analysis must be made to enable a firm to capitalize on opportunities perceived in the firm's environment. The analysis provides the basis for winning a battle for a particular market. To do so, however, this self-analysis must be realistic. It must be objective and deal with the realities of the situation, not how one would like it to be. A solid review of the firm's business, both past performance and present position, is critical to effective strategic planning.

How to Accomplish the Analysis

How should one go about this review? Conceptually, it is very simple and pedagogically fulfilling to talk of such a review. But how is it accomplished? The starting point is to decide in what business the firm is competing. Although this sounds very simplistic, it really is not. The traditional example is that of the railroads. Had the railroads realized several decades ago that the business they were in was the broader business of transportation and not just the narrower railroad business, they would have realized the inroads that other competitors were making in their business of transportation. The basic point is that a railroad competing against other railroads will reflect different corporate behavior from that of a railroad competing with other transporation companies such as airlines, barge companies, and railroads. Corporate objectives would be different; corporate strategies for achieving those objectives would be different. The business review would certainly show a different set of key skills and resources as well as a different subset of unique skills and resources. It short, the entire focus of the organization and its resources would be affected by the more precise definition of the business in which the railroad company competed.

Once that very basic decision has been made, the performance of the firm should be analyzed. Performance of the firm should be measured against that of other firms in the same market for the past three to five years. Performance should be initially measured in the broadest sense. What has been the growth in net earnings over this period? What has been the growth in market share? How have sales grown over this period? What return on investment has the company achieved over this period? What has been the experience of similar firms in the same market? What do these trends show you about your firm and its ability to compete in this market, as evidenced by the broad performance measures of the past? Based on the trends in the past and recent data, what is the position of the company now?

Does an analysis of this information actually show that the firm has been able to compete very effectively with some very good, if not unique, skills and resources?

Who Should Accomplish the Analysis?

More than any one thing, an effective self-analysis for the purpose of defining unique skills and resources must be performed by personnel with a detailed knowledge of the industry, of the more impressive competitors, and of their own company. While we have outlined some basic steps in searching for those unique skills and resources, it is indeed a complicated undertaking. The self-analysis must be rigorously carried out, but in many ways it is as much an art as a science. For one not completely familiar with the industry, the competition, and one's own firm, small competitive nuances would be lost. This substantial analysis could not occur because in the construct of strategic planning, we build upon this business review and eventually allocate scarce resources based on the findings of this review. The review can be made by anyone. An effective business review, which provides the basis for some tough management decisions, should be made by some of the most experienced personnel within the company and subjected to intense screening by top management. The assumptions that must be made and the attendant decisions that are an integral part of this analysis should be reviewed by top management because of their impact both on the corporate strategy and on the ultimate existence of the company.

Importance of Personal Values

Another important factor in an analysis of a company is the personal values of top management and the remaining personnel. The objective of the planning process is to develop corporate strategies that will take advantage of specific opportunities in the firm's environment by building upon key unique skills and resources of the firm. However, to be able to effectively marshall all the different resources and skills of the corporation requires a knowledge of the personal values and aspirations of the people who make up the firm. To develop an effective corporate strategy and then to effectively implement it, the goals and aspirations of the company personnel must be parallel with the strategy developed for the firm. This very personal appraisal is no less important, since the strategy finally chosen will be implemented by the personnel of the firm. To have a new strategy call for a significant group of individuals to work 60 hours a week for some time makes little sense if one knew that the particular group valued free time much more than effectively competing in a new market. In the same vein, it behooves a group little to come up with a strategy with broad social impacts if top management has very strong feelings against such social endeavors. The company's self-analysis must be realistic, thorough, and objective. Yet of equal importance are the personal values and aspirations that must make the strategy work.

4 Environmental Analysis

Importance of Environmental Analysis

One of the most critical aspects of strategic planning (and, in fact, a major reason for it) is found in appraising the firm's environment. Strategic planning has become a very fashionable function of business management in the past decade. However, one wonders why it is of such recent vintage. Did firms not plan strategically in the 1940s and 1950s, or are we again taking a new phrase and applying it to an old management concept? No, one of the major reasons that firms did not, in fact, (in most cases) plan strategically is that their environment has changed dramatically only in the past few years. Change, particularly the rate of that change, has increased measurably. What had been taking a number of years to occur now may happen in a number of months. Now the firm must be more aware of these changes in its environment and, more important, must make an effort to use that information to determine long-range actions. The ultimate goal is to impact that environment and change it to the advantage of the firm.

Strategic planning has been accomplished in a variety of firms and with a variety of methods in the United States in the past, but now one single aspect is overriding. To be successful in the long run, a firm must use strategic planning techniques to operate effectively and efficiently. Gone are the days when top management across American industry survived and operated effectively simply because they had an ongoing business which continued to show an impressive growth record because of factors outside their control, such as the normal growth of the economy.

The analysis of the firm's environment becomes a critical part of the overall schema called strategic planning. Each firm exists in certain subsets of the overall environment of this large country. These subsets are, in many respects, similar if not identical. However, many firms in the same industry also exist in environments which may be very different from one another and consequently require different top management action and attention. Also, many firms in the same industry may have already found much different methods of competing more effectively because of basic differences in size, geographical location, attitude of management, ownership (family or publicly owned), etc. Because of these differences, the formulation of corporate strategy is a very individualistic undertaking. What is good for one company in one industry may be very different from what is good for a very close competitor. The assumption should not be made lightly that company A is not formulating and implementing an effective corporate strategy just because it does not, on the surface, appear to be analogous to some of the more successful firms in the industry.

Although a list of exhaustive and definitive environmental areas cannot be made for all firms, a number of areas must be considered for most firms: (1) economic, (2) technological, (3) social, (4) political, and (5) ecological. The firm's environment in these five areas should provide a good basis for determining the specific environmental trends that are significant.

The role of environmental analysis in strategic planning is twofold. The major and positive role is to determine specific opportunities available to the firm in its environment. This determination will provide the basis for the firm's top management to utilize their assessment of the key skills and resources and apply it to the specific opportunities available. The secondary and negative role is to warn the firm of occurrences in the environment which may threaten its future. With such an early warning system or a sensor of negative trends, the organization can more effectively take action to either change the trends in the environment or, lacking capability to do that, take management steps to minimize the negative impact on the firm.

Economic Environment

The economic environment is critical to most firms in the process of strategic planning. The analysis of this environment may be the most difficult to accomplish in many cases. In this analysis, the firm must deal with what is going to be occurring in the national economic scene. Just as the average firm can do little to impact what will be happening to the prime rate or the way the Federal Reserve manipulates the money supply of the nation, the average firm is very concerned about what actually does occur and its potential impact on the ongoing business of the firm.

Suppose you have a long-range construction program which you must accomplish in the next seven years. Then your analysis of the economic environment should provide a mechanism to decide whether you would be better off to accomplish the required financing now if the long-term rates are very favorable or to wait until the term structure of interest rates, which you have no control over, shifts dramatically by the time the funds will be required.

Depending on the basic lines of business in which a firm engages, various economic aspects are crucial to the existence of the firm. Some years ago, the carrying of extra inventory was not so onerous from a financial viewpoint. Recently, however, with the increasing cost of capital and the prime rising to the neighborhood of 12 percent, firms are using 24 to 36 percent annual rates as the overall cost of carrying inventory. Many firms have from 20 to 30 percent of the assets of the firms tied up in inventory. Consequently, the economic analysis of the environment and its impact on the firm's balance sheet and profit and loss statement is increasingly important.

A number of economic trends are of interest to a variety of businesses. Some environmental trends include the stability of the U.S. dollar and the impact of currency reevaluations; the projected growth in the gross national product; the expected growth in the wholesale price index; the expected growth in the consumer price index; the expected changes in depreciation guidelines; the expected changes in the investment tax credit; the cost of raising capital by issuing bonds; the cost of raising capital by issuing preferred stock; the cost of raising capital by issuing convertible preferred stock; the cost of raising capital by issuing common stock; the price-earnings ratio of common stock; the changes in the federal income tax structure; the changes in the state income tax structure; the changes in the average tax rates on real property; the expected changes in the social security tax; the expected changes in investor expectations of corporate securities as affected by increased rates of inflation in the economy; anticipated changes in the rate of unemployment in the United States, and a variety of other economic considerations.

Technological Environment

To many firms, environment in a technological sense is equally important. In this area particularly, the past decade has seen sharp increases in the rate of change. Thus, firms must be aware of and able to cope with these increasing rates of change. Whereas in many cases the firm is unable to cope most effectively with the information available in the economic environment, many times the firm is quite able to cope with the technological environment. Many firms that either have been built or have prospered and grown as a result of orientation to a certain technology are more able to understand and analyze the effects of changes in the technological environment. Some firms have a well-developed insight into the events of their technological environment but are unable to take advantage of that ability in a total economic sense. In that case, some of the unique ability to pin down specific opportunities in the technological environment would be considered as a skill available for trade to another firm to enable a better treatment of the critical economic environment.

Here, unlike many of the environments in which the firm must exist, the firm has greater opportunity to impact and change the environment. If a small firm spins off from an industrial giant and undertakes a development to which the industrial giant did not want to allocate resources (for a variety of good reasons), our system of competition would have that small, young firm playing a major role in the technological environment.

A number of technological trends may be of interest to a firm, but many of these will be industry-specific. Some that have broader applicability involve future changes in micro circuits, future changes in high-performance metal alloys, the long-run impact of solar heating, whether coal gasification will be an effective energy source in the next twenty years, what economic methods will ensure sources of fuel in the next decade, whether there are processes in the formative stages that will make obsolete current processes, the existence of certain methods of data automation that will change significantly, and a variety of other technological considerations.

Social Environment

In the coming decade, there may be no more important and rapidly changing environment for a firm than the area of social attitudes and values. As opposed to the past, when many attitudes and values could be taken for granted and action taken accordingly, many of these may be subject to major change. Social attitudes and values are changing in several crucial ways. First, the attitude of the individual and his or her relationship to the firm are changing significantly. No longer is it so easy to achieve goal congruence between the individual and the firm. No longer is it easy to get all employees to work overtime when it is necessary to get out a rush job. Employees have a broader continuum of interest, and the singular attraction of more dollars to take care of their needs is not necessarily sufficient in many present-day instances. The lure of leisure time and the attendant interest in the four-day week will provide many challenges to the industrial firms in the next decade. Second, as the complexion of the population changes, their expectations regarding the basic role of business in our economy and our way of life will change. It may be anticipated that public criticism of large business organizations will increase and that the public will become more distrustful of these large organizations. Third, as the changes become apparent across a broad segment of the population, more of the challenge and responsibility for improving social conditions that had been previously accepted in this country will be passed on to large business organizations for correction.

Since, in one simplistic construct, a business organization is little more than a collection of individuals working for the common good of the corporation, the social attitudes and values of the population of the next ten years are a critical variable in the long-run effectiveness of the successful corporation. As this issue ascends in importance, the organizational structures and systems must be modified to deal with this problem effectively.

Trends in the social environment that are of broad interest include the following: (1) the demand for more disclosure in the future from business organizations; (2) the demand for more disclosure in the future from government organizations and the attendant complication of providing company proprietary information that has been properly protected in the past but now, due to the Freedom of Information Act or some other basis of "sunshine government," can no longer be protected; (3) the increasing demand on government regulatory bodies to take a more active role in regulation in the public good and require a much more relevant, positive standard of performance than before; (4) public criticism of business' means of competition, such as advertising; and (5) the whole area of "quality of life" will be given more attention and provide both risks and specific opportunities in the social environment of the firm.

Political Environment

The political environment provides yet another critical variable in the long-run efficiency of a firm. As the United States evolves, the government has steadily become more involved in the regulation of firms. The regulation continuum is broad. On one end, there are highly regulated companies almost completely dependent upon one type or another of government regulatory agency. And, on the other end, we have totally unregulated industries that still have to comply with many government laws, regulations, and administrative procedures. This is just one more environment of a United States firm whose influence over the current actions and potential alternatives for the future is growing.

Some firms in regulated industries must necessarily be greatly concerned about the occurrences in the political environment. Not only must they be aware of trends in the environment, but they must also be able to effectively deal with, and to some extent shape, that environment. However, the more significant trends are extant at the other end of the continuum. Firms that several decades ago were in unregulated or minimally regulated industries now are finding themselves more and more concerned with trends in the political environment. The country is going through a political change; attitudes, and therefore behavior toward business, are changing. The average industrial company will have to face increasing government regulation and intervention.

Trends in the political environment that are of broad significance include the following: government policy toward corporate income taxes; and industrial concentration; policy toward the retirement age, equal opportunity, OSHA, pension funds, interlocking directorates, and interest rates; increasing involvement of citizen public interest groups; greater difficulty in obtaining permits from government agencies (e.g., nuclear construction permits); increased difficulty in the utilization of natural resources; and a variety of other political considerations.

Ecological Environment

It would be hard to find a specific environment of the firm which has grown more in importance during the past decade than the ecological environment. Few firms during the early 1960s tracked the trends and opportunities in this environment. Consequently, rapid change in this environment and its large impact on the firm are an example of precisely why strategic planning is required.

The firm today must carefully plan capital budgeting projects with one eye on environmental impact. Millions, yes billions, of dollars will be spent by industry in the next few years to reduce and eliminate practices and processes that are harmful to the environment. No longer is a proposed project solely measured on the "bottom line" with little or no consideration of its environmental impact.

The firm's ecological environment, in may cases, will be extremely difficult to analyze. It will be hard to identify specific trends and opportunities because of the stage of maturity of the environment. Agreed-upon standards have not been established. There are many opinions on a great many issues in this ecological environment, but standards are difficult to establish and utilize. Too long, in some perceptions, we have utilized solely economic yardsticks. Now we are having a hard time comparing ecological benefits with economic ones.

Trends in the ecological environment that are of broad interest include the following: discharge requirements to fresh, coastal, and ground waters are becoming more rigid; pressure to establish company goals of near-zero environmental impact is mounting, original emission standards will gradually be broadened; emission standards will require that more pollutants be kept out of the atmosphere; more groups will utilize the court system to stop projects on environmental grounds; entirely new industries will appear in the next decade based on the changes in the ecological environment that were not conceived of in the 1960s; after large successes have been attained in the areas of water and air pollution, major efforts and attendant successes will be made in the area of noise pollution; and the concepts of social cost and social benefit will become common standards by which major projects are measured.

Summary

There are few things as certain as change itself. How the firm perceives that change, reacts to it, and acts to change its environment is a critical aspect of strategic planning and successful management. There is a place for operational efficiency, but an efficient operation must fail if there is no longer a need for its output. The company that sits in an ivory tower as the world changes around it, and does not interact with and react to that environment, will find the ivory tower is its casket.

5 Corporate Assumptions

Planning in the firm requires a consistent basis. That basis is provided by corporate assumptions. While strategic planning is an objective of most well-managed firms, the methods used to achieve this objective may vary significantly. Corporate assumptions are an integral part of most strategic planning systems and a critical part of all effective strategic planning systems. The reasons for this are quite clear.

The planning function and the responsibility for its effectiveness are somewhat elusive. When line managers are told they have substantial responsibility for strategic planning in a firm, they sometimes have difficulty seeing past the first year which has to be accomplished for operational purposes. Consequently, when they have an opportunity to contribute less to strategic planning, they may well do so.

Types of Assumptions

An effective set of corporate assumptions is a major step toward resolving one major area of confrontation. Corporation assumptions provide an effective basis for strategic planning throughout the company. Just as initiating any program across organizational lines is difficult in a large company, trying to establish strategic plans with a time horizon of five to ten years can be exceedingly difficult.

Corporate assumptions should be of two basic types. The first type encompasses assumptions that are sufficiently broad to be developed by most companies, notwithstanding the company size or industry. Examples of this first type would be political trends, economic conditions, technological change, and social attitudes.

The second type of corporate assumptions are much narrower and unique to the company with a formal planning system. Examples of this second type might be fuel resources or electric system growth for a public utility. As strategic planning matures as an integral function of business, movement from the second unique type of corporate assumption can be expected. Several years ago, how many long-range plans (not involving public utilities) were concerned with the problems inherent in fuel resources compared with today? Strategic planning can provide the greatest benefit when uncertainty of the future is high. Yet research has shown that in those areas where uncertainty is highest, planning is the most difficult and is either delayed for long periods or never formally accomplished at all.

Political Trends

It may have been possible for industry to disregard significant trends in the political world several decades ago, but that time is long past. What is occurring in the political environment today and what this portends for the future may have dramatic impacts on how a company will compete in the future. Corporate survival, in ever-increasing numbers, is controlled by the evolving political system in which we live.

Consequently, corporate assumptions involving where we are today in the political environment and where we are going in the future are vital to most, if not all, United States industry. What assumptions are extant about the degree of government regulation in the future? What will the government's corporate income tax be in the next five years? What changes will occur in the investment tax credit program? Will the federal government's program for environmental safety change in the next five years? What percentage of the workforce will be required to be female, black, Hispanic, etc., in the next five to ten years? Will the Democratic majority in Congress and the decided Democratic electorate in the United States monopolize United States politics and consequently United States political action and decision making for the next decade?

These questions may have varying political significance to different companies. Answers to some of them may be critical to firms engaged in industries requiring a large investment in plant and fixed assets. Obviously each question cannot be answered with certainty. However, arriving at a corporate position on the key political considerations provides multiple benefits to a progressive company. The alternatives available to a company that perceives a shift in political emphasis several years before it occurs may be many more than those available to a company that waits until the change occurs. It is a common saying that "Top management does not like surprises." There is much truth to that, and its existence provides a rationale for a strategic planning system. Even though top management may not always be able to react much differently to a significant change in the political environment, advance warning and the consequent more reasoned analysis will permit a much more meaningful decision process.

One of the more basic benefits accrues simply from the development of the corporate assumption on political trends. As the assumption is developed and evolves through iteration in the organization, the mere existence of this corporate assumption process will be beneficial to the firm. Many line and staff managers will be exposed to the problems and concerns developing in this area of business. Some of these, though good managers, will never have thought of the consequences and ramifications of some of the trends discovered, ratified, and published as a corporate assumption in the political environment. With the establishment of a system that routinely, yet specifically, develops these corporate assumptions involving the appropriate personnel in the company, the company's current operations will benefit and strategic planning will be enhanced.

Economic Conditions

While political trends may not have overriding significance to all firms, it would be difficult to find one not concerned with economic conditions. Granted, some firms will be more or less concerned with macroeconomic concerns in the United States than others, but in one way or another economic conditions are a very basic concern of industry.

What will the inflation rate be for the next 10 years? What will be the movement in the term structure of interest rates? Will the prime rate drop below 5½ percent in the next five years? What will the normal price-earnings rate movement be over the next 10 years? Will the current high unemployment affect the labor force in the next 10 years?

The answers to these and other key economic questions provide an economic basis for plans developed by firms. If capital budgets require substantial outlays in the next 10 to 15 years, the cost and availability of capital as well as the internal funds flow will be crucial to effective decision making.

Technological Change

Corporate assumptions involving technological change are often among the most critical in many industries. One of the most pressing reasons for strategic planning in the last decade has been the increased rate of technological change.

The determination of how a firm will compete is an integral part of the firm's corporate strategy. Several decades ago, technological change was occurring at a relatively fast pace in some industries but not across the continuum of industries. In the watch industry the rate of technological change has been slow; consequently corporate strategies were easily formulated and implemented for more than 300 years. This has undergone a dramatic upheaval in the past ten years and effective corporate strategies have been evolving almost as quickly as annual reports.

Equally rapid technological change has been extant in other parts of the nation's economy, such as microelectronics, even though the industry history is much shorter.

The data processing industry, which has had far-reaching effects on United States industry, hardly existed three decades ago. New series of equipment which initially took up to ten years to develop and deliver are coming off the line now in less than five years. Rapid technological change has occurred in this industry, and in return this industry has hastened technological change in United States industry.

How will the basic technology underlying an industry change in the next five years? What technology, yet unknown, will change the entire industry in 10 to 15 years? What percentage of overall budgets will companies spend for research and development in the next decade? How will the existence of technological change affect concentration ratios within the industries?

The answers to these and other equally difficult questions involving technological change are vital to more and more United States industrial firms. The rate of technological change cannot be discounted or ignored. Relevant assumptions must be made about future changes in technology.

Social Attitudes

The area of social attitudes and human values is also becoming increasingly important to our economy. No longer can long-range strategies be effectively established which do not take into consideration the basic reactions of company personnel. The work ethics and behavior responses taken for granted in the past must be dealt with much more explicitly and less circumspectly now.

Will continued migration to California continue for the next ten years? What will be the attitude toward more married women entering the workforce? Will the majority of United States industry be on a 4-day, 40-hour week in ten years? What are the prospects for "flexitime" in the future? Will the increasing age of the population require new methods of utilizing old, underutilized human resources? Will the aging of America require totally new concepts in the care and comfort of elderly Americans? What are the consequences of the steadily increasing United States divorce rate on the markets of the future? Will the initiatives toward zero growth take hold in the next decade and pose major problems to sustained economic growth? What are the implications for your business of a less mobile workforce that requires more personal time? The answers to these and other questions involving social attitudes and values are critical to a majority of United States industry today.

In discussing less general (but no less important) corporate assumptions, the unique situation of the company must be considered. While the more typical, broad assumptions have applications across most firms, usually each firm must develop some narrower assumptions that fit its specific environment.

A good example of such an assumption is the case of fuel resources. Five to ten years ago, corporate assumptions about fuel resources in any industry but public utilities would have been something of a rarity. Fuel—not only its availability but also its price—was pretty much taken for granted. Public utilities had detailed corporate assumptions because fuel was a major cost item to them. Fuel also provides an array of alternatives by which the utility can change its corporate strategy and compete more effectively. For instance, some major utilities in the past decade have made major commitments and investments to utilize nuclear power generating equipment. Others have made major commitments to coal. With other alternative fuels, such as gas and oil, they provide a wide array of alternatives. Not only the questions of availability and cost must be addressed, but also the increasingly important side effects of pollution.

However, with the events in the international oil scene of the past several years, fuel resources are becoming more vital to much of United States industry. With the gas shutoffs experienced in various parts of the country during the winter of 1977, fuel has become a most critical variable. That a firm effectively analyzes its environment and develops specific opportunities is of little positive benefit if the effective corporate strategy fails in implementation because of a gas shortage. Strategy formulation is only one important facet of corporate strategy, yet many times the bulk of the effort is placed in strategy formulation. However, any effective corporate strategy must be able to be implemented.

Consequently, companies are putting more emphasis on the fuel required to run plants and factories. Depending upon the area of the country and how the industry is fueled, effective long-range plans must take into account fuel problems. The degree to which this has become a critical item is evidenced by the increasing number of firms that are now exploring for natural gas and oil reserves. The criticality of the problem of fuel resources varies widely, but fuel is becoming a more important subject in the strategic planning process.

Another example of a more narrow corporate assumption might be one on human resources. The data processing field has been expanding so rapidly that it is extremely difficult to get sufficient trained personnel. High growth rates cannot be sustained unless adequate personnel are available to sustain that growth. Consequently, a firm in that industry must develop corporate assumptions about what will develop in human resources during the next five years. Depending upon its analysis, the firm may discover that in order to provide sufficient trained personnel for its planned future growth, unusual options must be taken now.

Depending upon the industry in which a firm competes, geographical location, size, product line, and other critical variables, there may be several unique areas where specific corporate assumptions should be developed. These assumptions will provide a basis for future strategic plans.

Responsibilities

The ultimate responsibility for strategic planning in a firm must rest with top management. Without their personal support and involvement, even detailed efforts at effective strategic planning will eventually be relegated to an inconsequential role. However, some portion of the organization must initiate the assumptions and coordinate and monitor their development. In many large organizations, this function will be accomplished by a corporate planning staff. In some large organizations, they are given the responsibility to coordinate the formulation, review, and approval of corporate assumptions.

Depending upon the firm's internal organization and the breadth and depth of talent located in the corporate planning staff, their role may vary considerably. In some well-staffed organizations, they may have the requisite talent to initiate the assumptions and then control the review and approval process. It is more likely, however, that in many organizations they will have a coordinating role. Corporate planning personnel will make sure that the responsibility for developing the corporate assumptions is firmly assigned, and then they will coordinate the review and approval process. No matter what the involvement of corporate planning personnel, one consideration should be paramount. Corporate assumptions should be reviewed and/or developed by the most knowledgeable personnel in that area in the company. Some of the corporate assumptions are tenuous at best because of the increasing uncertainty that we must deal with. It makes little sense, therefore, to leave the major responsibility of developing the basis for a strategic planning system to chance or ill-informed personnel. A firm's dedication to strategic planning is sometimes difficult to gauge in some areas. It does not take long to determine whether a firm's corporate assumptions were developed by someone as a rush project or are well-thought-out predictions made by the appropriate people in the firm. Overall, strategic planning without top management support and emphasis is not effective. The same can be said for the corporate assumption portion of strategic planning.

Timing

The timing of corporate assumptions depends a great deal on their substance. Some corporate assumptions might be so time-sensitive that they would need be updated on a quarterly or monthly basis. However, most corporate assumptions are updated semiannually. They provide the basis for the strategic planning process and then are updated semiannually. Since we will usually be dealing with formal planning systems with at least a three- to five-year planning horizon, updates more frequent than semiannually will not be required.

6 Corporate Objectives

After it has been determined that certain of the firm's skills are unique and that specific opportunities are available in the rapidly changing environment, top management has the task of setting corporate objectives. These objectives are the visible endpoints which have been established for the firm and which focus on what the company expects to achieve during future operations. Should a distinction be made between goals and objectives? A distinction can be made if one chooses to, but in this book the terms will be used synonymously.

Characteristics

Conventional wisdom has generally shown that the objectives must be set from the top down. Then the plans to meet these corporate objectives are established from the bottom up. These corporate objectives must have a variety of qualities if they are, in fact, to provide the level of corporate attention and concentration intended. First, corporate objectives must be measurable. The corporate objective is a visible standard against which the progress of the company can be measured. In fact, measuring corporate objectives can be very difficult in some areas. In normal areas such as objectives for profitability, sales, share of market, or return on investment, finite measures of performance are relatively easy to apply. However, as one moves from the quantitative into more qualitative areas, the question of measurability, though no less important to the long-run efficacy of the firm, becomes exceedingly thorny. Consequently, one of the important tasks of top management is to see that corporate objectives provide measurable standards of corporate performance.

Second, corporate objectives must be specific. It is obviously less than satisfactory to have corporate objectives that say "It is the objective of this company to be profitable." Needless to say, few companies would argue with the objective, as far as it goes. However, a corporate objective provides guidance to the corporate family. This particular corporate objective provides very little guidance. If it instead stated "The objective of this company is to attain a 10 percent compound growth rate in earnings per share for the next three years," then the managers of the company would have a much more definitive standard by which to evaluate specific project alternatives. In some cases, very general corporate objectives may have value, but specificity, although difficult in some cases, generally must be achieved.

Third, corporate objectives must form the apex of a hierarchy of objectives. Corporate objectives focus on what is important for the firm to achieve. Just as there are corporate objectives, it follows that in the hierarchy of objectives there will be department or division objectives, which will support and contribute to the fulfillment of the corporate objectives. To accomplish these department and division objectives, the managers must have sufficient resources. These lower-level objectives will be accompanied by an allocation of personnel, material, and capital resources, in ultimate support of the corporate objectives. In many firms, resources including the total spectrum of men, money, and material are often spent with no recognizable impact on or support for objectives set by top management. The establishment of corporate objectives is an attempt in the management process to focus the company's increasingly scarce resources to achieve those tasks deemed most critical by top management.

Corporate objectives should also bridge the gap between long-range and short-range plans. At this point we shall not try to make distinctions between long- and short-range plans. However, it should be noted that corporate objectives can and should include elements of both. The objectives should not all be out three to five years because by the time the measurements are complete, the answer may well be irrelevant. However, the objectives should also not all be so short-term that the tendency to "put out brush fires and concern oneself with day-to-day management" is reinforced by the very management process of strategic planning that is intended to force line management to think more strategically and less operationally. Behavior modification must be reinforced and approved when a rational amalgamation of long- and short-range objectives is achieved. There are too many good and valid reasons why line management lives in a short-run and "brush fire" world to reinforce that behavior with a strategic planning system.

Responsibility

Corporate objectives are a key management responsibility. The establishment and definition of corporate objectives cannot be effectively delegated. Top management carries certain responsibilities which, for good and valid reasons, cannot be taken on by others. Top management lives in an environment different from that of the other members of the firm. As a result, their outlook is bound to be different. How they perceive trends in the environment, based upon their experience and their ability is obviously different from how lower-level management perceives them. Although it is certainly the job of middle management to think like a top manager of the firm, it is extremely difficult to bring the same insights and attitudes to that assignment. Consequently, top management, with its broad responsibility for the long-run efficacy of the firm must assume this task. Just as the top managers of the firm have an overall view of the environment and the attendant skills and weaknesses of the company, the middle manager, by design, is responsible for a more narrow portion of the organization. In a functional organization, it is a major role of the general manager to play down the importance of any specific functional group for the optimization of the overall organization. Middle management cannot be expected to have a total corporate view and set objectives that would be as realistic and effective in all circumstances.

Contribution

But enough about what corporate objectives should be. What, in fact, do they contribute to the management of a firm in a rapidly changing environment? Corporate objectives serve the basic purpose of focusing the resources of the company. Strategic planning is a method of management that provides a means of providing emphasis. Many firms have been successful and show fine overall rates of return in the past through little or no correlation to the soundness of their management. Decision making in the firm did little to contribute to its long-run success. That time is changing. More and more, it is patently obvious that because of the critical nature of the next decade, the firm that makes the better resource allocation decisions and utilizes its human and financial resources in a more effective manner will be here in the 1990s. No, that is not to say that chance will never play a role in the success of a firm. That cannot be said. But it can be said that the role of management will be much more critical in the future than it has been in the past, and firms that have continued to succeed just because they existed will tend more to extinction. Resource allocation and an effective organizational structure to implement effective strategies are becoming increasingly important. Top management can no longer afford the luxury of various middle managers utilizing increasingly scarce resources if they do not, in fact, support the overall objectives of the corporation. Top management has no recourse but to be totally involved with the establishment, the changing of, the routine evaluation of, and the reporting of performance against corporate objectives if it is going to make its most substantial and vital contribution to the firm's operation.

Corporate objectives can take many forms. Some major companies do not have corporate objectives as such. They prefer to have objectives stated in various business plans within the company, but they do not formulate one set of overall objectives. They feel that by utilizing the objectives of the organizational units, they have more specific objectives. These specific objectives are then developed within the company. By doing this, they have a hierarchy of objectives that are very specific and generally more quantitative. On the other hand, some major corporations have very established, specific corporate objectives which, in fact, drive the total corporate planning system.

Corporate objectives are an integral part of a strategic planning process. They are provided by top management and focus on action and resource allocation throughout the firm. To be effective, they must be specific, verifiable, measurable, and current. They are one of the cornerstones of an effective strategic planning process.

7 Corporate Strategy

Definition

In this chapter we will be concerned about the strategy of an organization. A definition of strategy is a good place to start. If you look up the word in a dictionary, you will find that the word *strategy* derives initially from a military meaning. It means

The science of planning and directing large-scale military operations specifically, of maneuvering forces into the most advantageous position prior to engagement with the enemy.[1]

Although this definition is not one that we will continue to use, it has much to offer for a concept of strategy in a business sense. Top management in the firm has the responsibility of maneuvering its forces (the resources of the firm) into the most advantageous position prior to engagement with the enemy. It might not be quite appropriate to say that General Motors and Ford are enemies, but they certainly take up different positions on the economic field of battle each year when their new lines come out. It also may not be appropriate to call computer firms like Control Data Corporation, Honeywell, and Burroughs enemies; but when IBM is ready with a new generation of equipment, the field of battle is set for some years to come. The definition of military strategy provides a good base on which to build a concept of business strategy. This is particularly true since the concept of corporate strategy is comparatively new while military strategists have been plying their trade for centuries.

By a corporate strategy, we mean the mix of policies and strategic plans that will enable a firm to achieve the objectives established. The objectives tell where the firm is going and when it is going to get there. Corporate policy and strategic plans fill in how the firm will accomplish its objectives and specifically what the firm will do to reach them. A *strategy* is a specific action that a firm will take to achieve an objective. It is usually coupled with the allocation of resources required to achieve the objective. A firm may have an objective to increase market share of a certain product by 25 percent in two years. A strategic plan would be developed that incorporated that objective. The plan would have (1) those individuals responsible for carry-

39

ing out the plan, (2) the resources required to accomplish the plan, (3) the time frames involved, (4) the method of measurement to ensure that progress was being made toward the objective, and (5) much more detail that is involved in a strategic plan.

Examples

But what, then, is the strategy of the firm in achieving that objective? The strategy that the firm pursues may take on many different aspects. One strategy the firm might adopt is to change its make versus buy decision. Whereas previously a major portion of the product had been subcontracted, now the company would make the item internally. This might allow the company to make a substantial investment in facilities in order to reduce the cost of the items and be able to compete for a larger market share with a more efficient production base. Another strategy might be for the firm to change the quality of its product in order to increase its market share. Still another strategy might be for a firm to change the manner in which its product is serviced. The industry may never have emphasized service in the past, and yet by doing so, the firm could substantially increase its market share. Strategy, then, is simply a plan or an action to achieve an objective.

Strategies can be of many different types. Strategies usually deal with the allocation of the physical resources of a firm. However, some strategies can deal with the personnel assets of a firm. A company in a high-technology area might well deal as much in strategies that would concern their limited scientists and scientific personnel as in their physical resources.

Strategies generally, in one way or another, deal with the external environment. In the concept of strategic planning, the firm must analyze both its own unique skills and resources and the threats and opportunities in the external environment. Strategies must then be developed based on these analyses that will allow the firm to be competitive in the future. Strategies may have to be created for a variety of external reasons. The main competitor of a firm may make a move that must be countered. The political environment may change so dramatically that a change in strategy must be made. When a new item such as a transistor is developed, a firm may have to change its method of competition. A financial change in an external environment may cause a major change in a firm's strategy. Selling versus leasing computers was a major issue that had to be dealt with in the early 1950s.

Strategy can also be looked at from the viewpoint of the organization. It is common to talk about the concept of corporate strategy. By so doing, one is implicitly talking about the overall strategy of the corporation. The corporate strategy, however, may not be the only strategy. Particularly in a large decentralized company, there may be divisional strategies that exist because of the complexity of the overall corporate management process. The divisional strategies will be integrated (hopefully) into the overall corporate strategy.

One of the specific things that should be considered when describing a strategy is that portion of the strategy which is a business strategy and that portion which is a personal strategy. The role of general management in a firm requires top management to be responsible for and involved with strategic planning. However, because top management, from a personal sense, may be different from lower-level management, the decisions they make will reflect their backgrounds, aspirations, motivations, education, etc. Because of this difference, the general management point of view requires the general manager to lift himself or herself above the functional discipline that brings one to the executive suite. Hopefully it enables the general manager to contribute to the corporate decision-making process with the good of the entire organization high on the list of decision criteria. It may well be very difficult to distinguish where personal strategies end and business strategies begin. The general manager is said to integrate and effectively use the resources of the firm to take care of the threats and the opportunities in the external environment. It should not be hard to see that the integration of the manager's personal values and motivations may well be the governing part of the company's strategy.

Growth

Another consideration regarding strategy is that of growth. It almost seems that unless a company is growth-oriented in the United States, we think that there must be something wrong with it. Growth can be achieved in a variety of ways. First, growth can be achieved through either internal growth or diversification. Internal growth may be achieved through increased sales of the same product in already existing markets. The United States has provided a fertile field in this area, since we have grown as a total market both physically and economically. However, internal growth can also be achieved by selling new products in an already existing market. New product development may be a cornerstone of the competitive posture of a firm and allow it to achieve substantial growth results. On the other hand, some of the most significant growth patterns in United States industry have been the development of new products for markets that did not previously exist. An example of this would be nuclear power generating stations in the past few years.

Diversification

Diversification also provides a method of achieving growth. By diversifying into another line of business, a firm is able to acquire another firm in a different line and then effectively compete in that new line of business. The 1960s showed a great deal of growth for growth's sake with the advent of the conglomerate form of business. One theory behind that movement was that basic management skills were transferable and a wide variety of companies were acquired that were in totally different lines of business. The strategy worked in some instances, yet proved very ineffective in many others.

Integration

Vertical integration is another way to achieve internal growth. As a firm integrates forward toward the market or backward to the source of raw materials, growth can be achieved. Some of the most effective means of vertical integration have been those companies that have integrated back to the source of their fuel in the past decade before the energy crisis. Not only have those companies achieved a savings in the overall cost of their fuel, but in many cases they also have uninterrupted supplies of critical fuel when their competitors are closed down. Just as we cannot predict the future with certainty, there may be benefits derived from some logical strategies that far outweigh the original reasons for pursuing them.

If a strategy is an integral part of strategic planning, what is the best way to develop it? As with many other tasks, there is no one right way to develop a corporate strategy. One important way is to have an integrated corporate planning system. As the corporate planning system provides a method of more efficient resource utilization and allocation of scarce resources to meet the firm's objectives, it also provides a method for determining a strategy. The corporate planning process should require that plans be developed with appropriate strategies. There is no corner on the market of effective strategies in the executive suite. Just as the corporate planning process must permeate the company, so must the development of strategies flow the same way.

Research has shown that some of the most strategic decisions are made at middle management levels in companies where personnel know more about the competitive environment and realize what actions must be accomplished in a strategic sense. Just as the line management of a company must spend time on the strategic consequences of their actions, they must also spend time developing adequate strategies which will enable the firm to achieve the established objectives.

Strategic Business Unit (SBU)

During the 1970s, new approaches to the concept of strategic planning were developed. One of the most effective and widely used is the strategic business unit concept at General Electric. Several years ago, Mr. R. Gutoff, a Vice President of General Electric, gave a presentation on the SBU concept at the Graduate School of Business Administration of the University of Michigan. At that time he was in charge of strategic planning at General Electric.

SBUs were developed at General Electric because the 1960s had seen a large growth in sales with little growth in earnings per share and a significant reduction in return on assets. General Electric referred to that as a period of "profitless growth."

As a result of this profitless growth, GE decided it must develop a new concept to overcome this very serious problem. As a consequence, GE created a new concept of strategic planning. The SBU system developed there was derived, to some extent, from financial theory. GE decided, as a diversified firm, to manage its various organizations as a portfolio. There would be an overall corporate strategy, but each business unit would serve a clearly defined product/market segment. Each business unit would also have a well-defined strategy for its market segment that would be consistent with the overall requirements of the corporation but competitive and effective for the particular market segment.

The overall portfolio of business units, then, would be managed as a whole to eliminate the problems of growth without profitability. Growth would be achieved not only in sales but also in earnings per share and return on assets. In effect, the broadly diversified organizations that make up General Electric would be subjected to differentiated management to achieve overall corporate goals.

To implement the SBU concept, the organization must be broken into strategic units. This requires, in most organizations, a realignment of responsibility. Traditional management principles such as organizing on the basis of span of control are not controlling factors. Basic management decisions must be made, and the organization must establish as a primary objective the serving of a number of independent product/market segments in the most effective and efficient manner.

Next the market of the unit must be analyzed. The firm must decide two things: (1) the position of the strategic business unit in that particular market and (2) the long-term attractiveness of that market. Both these decisions can be made on a quantitative or qualitative basis. Generally, you will find elements of both. The relative market position of the business unit can be looked at as its market share coupled with a qualitative management estimate. The long-term attractiveness of the market can be based primarily on economic analysis.

Most companies combine the competitive position and industry attractiveness in a 2 × 2 or a 3 × 3 matrix to facilitate strategic management. Based on the cumulative quantitative and qualitative management inputs, a gradual differentiation of the various organizational elements is accomplished. This leads, then, to more realistically tailored management of these units.

In the past, many large firms managed all organization elements with the same general policies. Thus there was a wide variation in the way the units responded to this policy direction because of their different basic characteristics. If a strategic unit has little potential in an unattractive market, you would expect it to be managed differently, be provided with different resources, and even possibly be assigned a different type of manager. This is the basic power of the SBU concept. Even though much of the analysis and final element placing is relatively subjective, still a definite degree of differentiation occurs which allows the firm to allocate its scarce resources more effectively and compete more efficiently in its multiple markets.

This first example of a poor business position in an unattractive market does not merit a major commitment and is commonly called a "dog." In short, the firm will probably reap what it can from the business with no major resource commitment and eventually rid itself of the problem.

On the other hand, a business unit can be in an unattractive market but have a strong competitive position. These units, commonly called "cows," are important to the overall corporate strategy for they provide funds to support other elements of the portfolio that have better growth prospects.

Business units in an attractive market but with poor competitive positions are commonly called "sweepstakes" units. They may have the potential to develop into very profitable components of the corporate portfolio, or maybe they never could compete effectively with a sufficient market share to make major resource commitments worthwhile. The judgment of management must be heavily relied upon both to place the business units in their relative positions and to determine the risk/return potential of these sweepstakes units.

Business units in attractive markets with good competitive positions are commonly called "stars." These are managed for the long term and are supported in their cash needs by the "cows."

To name four different units is simply to identify the differences in the overall corporate portfolio of businesses. These units should grow in a different manner, be managed in a different manner, and return different streams of earnings to the organization over time. The characterization allows differentiation in the allocation and utilization of scarce resources, whether they be financial, physical, or managerial.

The essence of the General Electric SBU concept is simple yet very powerful. Possibly the greatest benefits to be achieved from the concept come not from the formulation of corporate strategy but from its implementation. The following information has been provided by General Electric in public sources.

(a) *Control*: SBU control systems with GE are based on key success indicators (called business screens). For each SBU, performance measurements are monitored on five broad criteria—market position, competitive position, profitability/cash flow, technological position, and external trigger points. Standards for each criterion are set and weighted differently, depending upon which category the SBU is classified as. In addition, a "quality of performance" ranking is maintained as a measure of how well individual SBU managers have attained their standards of performance. As one GE manager put it, "the maturity of our SBU planning process could be measured when we began to bridge the gap between budgeting and the strategic plan."

(b) *Measurement and Reward*: The measurement and reward of managerial performance was perhaps the biggest shift in the revised GE system. Under the previous system of reward, Ge had compensated key managers on the basis of residual earnings—controllable profits during the planning period less a charge for corporate services and capital. Under the SBU system, however, SBU managers in different sectors of the matrix are measured and compensated differentially according to the following bonus schedule.

SBU Classification	Current Performance (Residual Income)	Future Performance (Strategy)	Other Factors
Invest/Grow	40%	48%	12%
Selectivity	60%	28%	12%
Harvest/Divest	72%	16%	12%

(c) *Management Development*: Management development in GE has also shifted to reflect differential needs in differential business elements. Invest/grow business managers are developed to foster entrepreneurial characteristics. Cash cow (selectivity) business managers are developed to take sophisticated/hard looks at their businesses, and harvest/divest managers are developed with a heavy orientation toward experience/operations/cost-cutting. One GE executive pointed out the rationale for this developmental effort: "Nothing is more demoralizing than having the wrong [kind of] manager in the wrong job."

This information on the implementation of the SBU system provides some of the most valuable insights available in the implementation of strategic planning systems. Most companies have persistent problems with the need to compensate an executive in the short run for long-term performance. One of the basic problems with business management is that many times action must be taken in the short run for which economic benefits will only result later. Why should "overtaxed" line managers spend time on long-range strategic planning when they are compensated on short-term profitability? This General Electric system approaches that problem head-on with compensation being determined by the requirements of the SBU. This effectively integrates the executive compensation (and hopefully appropriate behavior modification) with the overall corporate strategy of the firm.

Of course, as in most complex issues, there are difficult problems still to be resolved. One such problem is the measurement difficulty inherent in pensating a manager on the basis of long-range contributions. However, this difficulty is well worth the long-term benefit. To achieve long-range contributions in a particular SBU, various plans and programs must be developed and implemented in the short run. They will not necessarily be profitable in the short run, but they are capable of being measured in that time span. Consequently, more effort must be expended in determining the manager's contribution to the long term by examining long-range strategies which are implemented in the current accounting period through a variety of actions, plans, and programs.

The General Electric SBU concept has been widely implemented in diversified corporations in the past few years. It provides a powerful approach to effective strategic planning in a diversified corporation.

Summary

Many tools and techniques may be used in the corporate planning process, but much of the iterative thinking that goes into developing an effective strategy must come from management. It is their job; and it is the one function most difficult to delegate because of the interrelationship of corporate purpose, mission, objectives, and values of top management.

Note

1. *Webster's New World Dictionary,* New York: The World Publishing Company, 1960, p. 1441.

8 Corporate Policies and Plans

The foregoing chapters have dealt with a variety of aspects of strategic planning. Now it is time to discuss the roles of both business policies and business plans.

Policies

A business policy is a general plan or statement that answers the question "How is the firm going to accomplish this objective?" It sets forth guidelines to daily decision making throughout the firm so that many decisions do not have to rise higher in the organization for resolution.

In providing operating guidelines for the entire organization, policies provide one of the basic coordinating devices or processes through which the diverse elements of the organization can be brought more effectively to bear on the firm's overall objectives. There may be several levels of policy in an organization. At the corporate level, policy statements will provide some insight into the thinking and decision process of the top executives of the organization. Then when problems occur during the normal work situation, middle managers have appropriate guidelines to rely upon. They will know that by treating a problem situation in a certain way, they are effectively marshalling the resources under their control in a manner that top management will approve. Their guidelines fill a very important role; they allow senior management to spend less time on certain management areas. Management by exception can be meaningful when lower-level managers can have a reasonably comprehensive set of corporate policies with which to operate.

There may be other levels of policy in an organization. Often there are cases where the requirements for divisional or departmental policy are substantial. Normally, the scope of these is less than that of the corporate policy, but they serve the same effective purpose. On their level, they provide the operating or functional manager with the guidelines for decision making in that job. When occasions arise where there might be some reluctance to make a certain decision because of a difference of opinion or reluctance to support a portion of the overall corporate objectives, lower-level policy may very explicitly tell middle managers what their responsibilities are and what degrees of freedom they have in resolving the situation. The purpose of a formal planning system is to more effectively marshall the resources of an organization to achieve overall corporate objectives. The corporate and lower-level policy statements are an effective way of accomplishing this.

There are several purposes of corporate policy. It provides guidelines which will assist in achieving more consistent decision making throughout the organization. By issuing a corporate policy, the executives of the organization can provide insight into their considerations and decision-making process and consequently allow lower-level management the benefit of executive-level leadership without moving the situation or the decision up the formal chain of command each time it arises. One of the basic management movements of this century has been the move to decentralization. More decisions have been moved lower in the organization where in many cases more information is available to deal with the decision, rather than trying to move the problem and the pertinent information surrounding the decision up through several layers of executives which all, in one way or another, view the problem and its environment in a slightly different way. Decentralization is facilitated by the issuance of policies which in themselves provide the basis for decision making lower in the organization.

Policies can be created in a variety of ways. Generally, there will be some initial requirement for them. The basic need may arise at various levels within the organization, or something may happen which top management wants to ensure does not recur. No matter where the need for policy develops, it will weave through the same iterative process before it is signed off as a basic policy. Of course, not all policy statements restrict lower-management initiative. Just as some policies may add new restrictive guidelines to a process before lower management can take certain action, many times the issuance of a policy reduces or eliminates restrictive guidelines that may have been impeding the attainment of important corporate objectives in certain areas.

How should a business policy be formulated? What should the policy formulation process include? Normally, organizations find that policies are more effective when managers and supervisors are involved in the formulation process. When managers find out that their experience and judgment are valued and their inputs are accepted (not just asked for and then not heeded), the policy formulation process is bound to be more effective. This stands to reason, for the end result is not, as some might argue, the formulation of the policy. The end result (that so many times is too transient) is that after the policy has been formulated, when lower-level managers encounter a situation in which the new policy is operable, they will remember that new policy and act accordingly. We are trying to develop a formal system that will more effectively allocate resources within the organization in response to ever-changing environmental requirements. The essence of an effective policy is that the middle managers not only understand the rationale for it but have been substantially involved in its development and consequently will support it when the time comes to affect the behavior of the managers of the organization.

One of the basic problems of managers on the way up in almost any large organization is to learn to view the world not from their own perspectives, but from the perspective of their superiors in the next echelon or two above. This is not to say that all managers must have only their superior's viewpoint. It is to say that many times we do not sufficiently understand the position of top management. Then we may make suboptimal decisions as far as the overall organization is concerned. We may think we are making optimal decisions, and in fact we could if we only took into account the subset of the organization within which we are operating. However, one of the most critical management accomplishments is to reflect more of a general management viewpoint in recommendations and decisions when it is the appropriate and correct thing to do. By being involved in a substantitive manner in the development of divisional, departmental, and corporate policies, middle management can better understand the requirements of the senior positions. This is particularly true when the nuances of these higher-level positions might never otherwise be communicated to managers striving to get ahead in the organization.

Business Plans

Plans are the part of the formal strategic planning system which specify what must be done to reach the objectives established by the corporation. Action must take place after the analysis of the environment has been completed; after a determination of the strengths and weaknesses of the organization has been made; after the planning assumptions have been reviewed and a variety of alternative strategies have been considered. The plan answers the question of what has to be done throughout that portion of the organization covered by the plan in order for the organization to reach its overall objectives. If we are making a plan for the finance function in an organization, the financial aspects of the organization, such as cash flow, debt/equity structure, future financing considerations, dividend issues, etc., would be covered. If the plan covered a purchasing function, it might cover such areas as new suppliers, vendor reliability, value analysis goals, inventory turn objectives, and other relevant considerations that would be, in the end, supportive of and necessary to the overall accomplishment of corporate objectives. If we were in an operating division of a large railroad company, we might have a plan covering the increase in passenger traffic, the improvement in rail beds, the increase in freight traffic from other than railway competition, and so on.

What do all these areas have in common? They all are concerned with very detailed functional or operational responsibilities that must be effectively carried out in order for the overall organization to achieve its objectives. In order for the top executives of the organization to fulfill the overall corporate objectives month after month and quarter after quarter, the myriad of personnel throughout the organization have to accomplish tasks which are spelled out in their language and are doable from their point of view. It may be a long way from the board room to the receiving dock or to the inventory picking clerk or to the expediter, but their behavior should support the corporation's overall objectives. Top-level executives are paid for many things. One thing they are not paid for is stock picking or routine expediting. Therefore, the system and processes which they implement in their organization must focus and channel the behavior throughout the functional groups of the organization so that the overall goals can be attained. The business plan does this. The tasks are set forth. Responsibility is assigned. Resources are provided. Reporting requirements are established. Followup is ensured. If the plan is not met, the reporting cycle will develop that bit of information and alternate action must be taken. The plan is the putty of the organization. It lays out in some detail how the lower organizations must accomplish certain well-defined tasks before the overall goals of the organization can be achieved.

Types of Plans

There are a variety of types of plans. Most organizations have a plan of relatively short range at the organizational or unit level. This may have a time span of one to three or four years. This plan is for the purpose of the organizational unit that develops it. From the overall corporate objectives, lower-level organizational objectives are established. These objectives establish the endpoints of the unit for which the plan is made. The unit must have a variety of tasks assigned to it in order to support the overall corporate objectives. The plan will lay out, in reasonable detail for monthly or quarterly tracking, specifically what must be accomplished during the reporting period. The plan will list the strategies to be used to accomplish the subunit objectives. The responsible official of the organizational unit will be listed, and in many cases there will be further divisions of responsibility to lower levels by name. The resources necessary to achieve the subunit goals are also listed.

This organizational plan or short-term plan assists lower-level managers in directing their organizations. It communicates the needs of their organizational units throughout the hierarchy of the organization. It also provides reviewing officials along the management chain of command with much substantive information about the unit for which the plan has been developed.

Another type of plan is a *program plan*. Recently, management has decided that we must use different techniques to accomplish very important or very difficult jobs rather than just allowing the normal functional organization to achieve the expected results. In some areas this is called *program* or *project management*, and in other areas it is called *matrix management*. Regardless of the semantic difference, the goal is to more effectively accomplish a task with very precise accountability and responsibility. Sometimes these are major projects which, if not completed effectively and efficiently, would mean the demise of the corporation. In other cases, they may be a new development that must be effectively nurtured early in its product life in order to more effectively prolong and lengthen its eventual contribution to the overall goals of the organization. In any event, the program plan focuses management's attention in a much different way from the organization plan. As the organization plan focused on an organization unit, the program plan focuses management attention on a program deemed sufficiently important to the company to provide intensified management attention. These plans may, and usually do, cut across many organizational boundaries. They are programs which, if neglected, would result in major problem areas for the organization in the future. The issues involved might affect the financial viability of the company or restrict the company's future capability to react to important environmental changes. Usually a major corporate resource would be involved.

9 Implementation

If the basic purpose of strategic planning is considered, it is little wonder that it is a time-consuming, complex process to formulate a successful strategy. Strategic planning, done effectively, should increase management efficiency throughout the organization and enable the firm to achieve its corporate objectives. It is a tool which allows the corporation to anticipate environmental change. It provides management a tool to respond effectively to changes in the environment or even potentially to mold environmental change, in some cases, to fit the company. The overall planning program provides a general sense of direction to managers throughout the company. However, this very straightforward listing of virtues makes one very large assumption.

Strategic planning without effective implementation is little more than a misplaced academic drill. Much time and energy has been spent emphasizing strategy formulation in the past decade. And rightly so, in many instances. We certainly cannot worry about the consequences of poor implementation initially if we lack a concept to implement. However, such is no longer the case. In the past five years, many major companies have initiated formal strategic planning systems. The overall benefit to the organization will, to a large extent, depend on how well it implements the strategy that has been formulated. Consequently, the subject of implementation will be discussed now. Just as the 1960s and 1970s were primarily concerned with the development and formulation of an effective corporate strategy, so the 1980s and 1990s will see many initiatives attempt to implement these corporate strategies more effectively and efficiently.

What, then, is the challenge of implementation? What must be accomplished by an organization if it is to achieve the benefits that have been developed through the effective strategy formulation process? Is implementation really a difficult challenge for the future, or is it simply putting our minds to it once we are satisfied with our skills in the strategy formulation process? Implementation cannot really be that much of a challenge since the real difficulty is determining what is going to happen in the environments in which we compete and what, in turn, our competitors will be doing. The following should shed some light on this difficult area of strategic planning implementation.

Implementation covers all those problems, indeed challenges, and many more. As we start being concerned about implementing corporate plans

53

throughout organizations, if the organizations are small, then the problems, of course, are relatively smaller. But as we grow in size and then become large, diversified companies, implementation grows exceedingly complex. Then we are talking about possibly 50 to 100 subunits of an organization, and the employees in those units may well number in the hundreds of thousands or even millions. It then becomes apparent how complex the problem of implementation can be in large organizations. If one of the basic purposes of a strategic planning system is to increase management efficiency and effectiveness and provide a sense of direction to all corporate managers, it is clear that to do that effectively across a widely diversified organization is indeed a challenge.

Structure

How do you implement a strategic planning system in an organization? Two basic issues must be dealt with in such a manner that the strategic planning systems provide the benefits that are available. The first basic issue is the organizational structure. One of the basic management tasks in any organization is to develop a structure which will assist management in achieving its objectives. Certain tasks must be accomplished to achieve the corporate strategy that has been developed through the strategic planning process. The tasks must be efficiently broken down and assigned to all parts of the organization that should be assigned responsibility for accomplishing a portion of that work. The work must be set up and the organizations so structured that the people in the organization will work together effectively to accomplish the goals of the organization. To do this, an efficient structure of roles must be initially established and then maintained and changed as the circumstances dictate. Unfortunately, from a practical standpoint, we are faced with one stark reality. There are many things that we do not know about the intricacies and complexities of business management. But whenever we really get confronted with a "high hard one," we can always rationalize that by a minor (or sometimes major) organizational change. We somehow magically increase the efficiency and effectiveness of the organizations, and off we go again. How many times have you been in an organization where, if there has not been a major organizational change or personnel shuffle in the past year or two, you just know that it is right around the corner? True, from a theoretical sense, we need to modify the organization from time to time depending on the changes that are made in our competitive environment. But I doubt that research would show that the fast rate of environmental change would support even one half of the major reorganizations that we routinely see in large organizations.

One of the basic principles of management, whether in an organization of ten people or a million plus, is organizing. In organizing, research by Chandler has shown that the organizational structure will be determined by the strategy of the firm. What does this imply? What is the relationship between the corporate strategy of the firm and the manner in which the firm is organized? Simply, the formulation of corporate strategy and the attendant goals of the firm will determine, to a substantial extent, what the organizational structure of the firm must be. If a firm decides to market a product in both the European and the United States markets, then some part of the overall organization must take responsibility for completion of the tasks involved. How that task is assigned, how performance is measured against plan, who receives what compensation, etc., are all part of the overall organization and the attendant structure and processes that must be established after the European goal is set.

The need for an organizational structure derives from the need for cooperation. When a number of individuals are working in the same organization for the same overall corporate objectives, they still carry with them vastly different personal objectives. Consequently, it is possible to more effectively accomplish the corporate goals with an effective organizational structure.

Tasks

The important tasks that must be accomplished by the organization must be identified. In an organization, a number of things must be done before the overall objectives of the organization are achieved. The identification of all these important tasks is the first key to determining the correct organizational structure. Tasks may be broken down into tasks that must be performed on a functional basis. It may be that tasks in some organizations will be performed more effectively on a geographic basis. Other functions may be identified that must be done by staff members in the organization. There are any number of ways to determine how the tasks necessary to achieve the objectives of the organizations are identified.

After the tasks have been identified, they must be ranked in some relative order of priority. Not all tasks that have to be accomplished in any organization, no matter how large or how small the organization, are of equal importance. Sometimes one of the harder assignments is really understanding which tasks in fact are the more important to the firm's long-run efficiency. Nevertheless, the relative importance must be determined and then accomplished in accordance with the priority established.

Once the priority has been established and the tasks are assigned to certain organizational groups, authority must be given to those groups. The assignment of the task responsibility is merely the beginning. The unit to which the task is assigned must have the authority that goes with the responsibility. In this chapter, we will talk almost exclusively about *formal* authority. By that I mean the authority which resides in the organization niche and not with the person who happens to be occupying that niche at any point in time. There are several theories of authority, such as the competence theory and the acceptance theory which generally rely on research and principles in the area of organizational behavior. However, there is no overriding need to develop these several theories of authority as long as we note that when tasks are decided, priorities assigned, and organization subunits established to deal with those tasks, the subunits must be granted sufficient authority to accomplish the tasks.

The organizational structure must provide for a very basic ingredient at all times. We will have a corporate purpose in our strategic planning system. The organizational structure must allow these tasks to be related back to the accomplishment of the corporate purpose. We are trying to achieve a consistency of approach throughout the organization. As the tasks are logically tied back into the purpose, the relation will be helpful, even mandatory.

One final caveat on organization structure: it must not be an end in itself. We are addressing the organization in detail since the basic idea we are trying to set forth is that the large group of persons in the organization will contribute and use their different skills to enable the organization to meet its objectives and fulfill its corporate purpose. Often it is hard to determine when a group is working more for the overall good of the organization or is just fulfilling some narrow, organizational subobjective. This is a danger that must be considered and dealt with swiftly whenever it is apparent in the rich organizational fabric that covers a large organization.

Coordination

Once the tasks have been defined and distributed for accomplishment throughout the organization, coordination must commence. The more we subdivide the tasks to make their accomplishment more efficient and more effective, the more we must be concerned with coordination of those subunits. If the tasks were all assigned to one unit, perhaps all that would concern us would be the efficiency of that subunit, and we could assume that the coordination within one subunit would not be that difficult. However, since we are talking about medium-sized and large United States corporations, we are talking about a major problem in coordination. Corporate strategy is at best understood quite differently by a number of persons in the same organization. In the same manner, the corporate purpose and goals also mean different things to different groups within the same organization. Consequently, the organizational units (1) must coordinate the actions of their members and (2) must themselves be coordinated, if in fact we are to achieve the objectives of the organization.

A variety of tools can be used for coordination of large organizations. Imbedded in any organization is one of the most important coordination tools—the hierarchy of the organization. The hierarchy shows the formal lines of authority and responsibility that permeate the organization. Authority is delegated throughout the organization when organizational discretion is invested in a subordinate by that subordinate's superior. As subordinates report up the chain of command to their superiors, they report to and through fewer and fewer people. It might be likened to a river flowing downhill, as different task groups accomplish their assigned tasks and then report the accomplishment up the organizational chain of command. As the reporting levels go higher and higher, the reports start to be accumulated and aggregated for further reporting. Eventually all the reports come to rest in one final office, that of the chief executive officer of the organization. Just as the principle of span of control provides guidelines for determining some logical number of people who should be working for a supervisor, depending on a variety of factors, when the results are passed back up the line, they are passed through an ever-slimmer pyramid. Since supervisors have a different view of the world and have the responsibility for their units, one of their primary management jobs is the coordination of the results of their small subunit. They are aware (or should be) that the ultimate objectives of the organization will be achieved only if the numerous subunits accomplish the tasks that are defined, subdivided, and assigned to them.

This, then, provides coordination throughout the organization as similar and dissimilar tasks are being accomplished. As the results pass through the organizational chain of command, it is not uncommon for what a lower supervisor thought to be a good piece of work to actually turn out to be something that must be redone if it will, in fact, support the corporate objectives. Why does this happen? Even in the best organizations, the dissemination and understanding of corporate goals and objectives are difficult at best. Not only are we dealing with a variety of managers with different functions and business interests, but we are also dealing with their individual likes and dislikes and their possible differing motivations and needs, both individually and in groups. Consequently, the task assignment down the authority chain and the movement of the results back up must be accompanied by a great amount of information transfer, many facts, many perceptions, and invariably a normal amount of just plain bad information for any number of valid reasons. We address the need for good communication skills in an organization because we are trying to generate positive activity from a very diverse group of individuals and groups to support the overall objectives. The heirarchy method is vital to strategic planning.

Another method for coordination of responsibility is the use of committees. Sometimes, the word *committee* connotes that few results are expected. However, when it comes to the problem of coordination, committees have a positive role in an organization. Many problems in a large organization are so large and complex that they may be too large for any one portion of the organization to effectively handle. Consequently, a committee will be formed with representation from all involved parties. A leader of the committee will be established. How the committee actually operates and achieves positive results will depend on a number of variables. However, when it comes to the assignment of varied tasks to different subunits of an organization, the use of a committee to achieve coordination is an effective method for strategic planning.

A task force approach could also be used to implement a strategic planning system. In utilizing a task force, certain ground rules are established for the organization. First, the mere establishment of the task force shows that sufficient attention has been given to the issue. Next, when a task force that has been granted a high priority is used personnel are aware that the objective to be accomplished has been enunciated (to a greater or lesser degree). The task force then utilizes and coordinates inputs from very disparate parts of the organization as it tries to further the implementation of corporate strategy.

Information System

After the organizational structure has been established, and tasks have been identified, assigned a priority and parceled out, a different type of need arises. This requires the design and development of an information system for the organization. As the organization increases in size and complexity, its informational needs also grow. As the tasks are subdivided and assigned to subunits throughout the organization, there must be some method to measure the progress made. Informational needs of management start to expand as the issues get more complex. The development of meaningful standards also becomes an issue.

To successfully implement a strategic planning system, informational needs exist for both internal and external information. Just as we need to know on a periodic basis what of importance has occurred during a specified time in the manufacturing area of an organization, for example, we also need to know what has occurred in the external environment. If we subscribe to the management-by-exception theory, we must still have information on what has occurred in order to know what exceptions have been made in the period of operation.

Knowledge of the firm's operating environment is essential, yes, even critical, to the firm's long-run survival. The variable of the external environment and the opportunities and threats provided by that environment are an integral part of the concept of formulating corporate strategy. Various departments of subunits of the firm deal with different parts of the external environment. Reporting systems must be established that will convert the intelligence derived from the external environment. Then that must be woven into the information available within the firm. The total informational needs of the firm become mammoth as the firm grows larger. The key to this area of information and informational systems is whether the manager is better off with the amount of information that a modern manager must cope with. Many managers have so much information at their disposal that they do not really know what it is they need to know to effectively manage their organizations. This is one of the modern-day management problems that has been "helped" by the advent of the Xerox and IBM machines. Managers must now develop the information systems that will assist, not hinder, them in successfully implementing corporate strategy.

Developing an organizational structure for a large organization is analagous to setting up a Christmas tree for your children. Once you have the tree (structure) in its stand in the livingroom, you have barely started. The star that must first be placed on the top of the tree is analogous to the corporate purpose. It sits there for all to see and provides a sense of direction. However, with just a purpose and a structure (tree), much remains to be done. The structure is just the beginning. One of the major items to be placed carefully on the tree are the lights. People in an organization are analogous to tree lights. Just as the lights must all play together to light up a Christmas tree, so must all the different individuals in an organization pull together to achieve what the corporation has established as meaningful goals. Just as each light and each Christmas ornament are different, each individual is a unique entity with different interests. Consequently, the organizational structure must be hung with various processes and systems to motivate human behavior to support the organizational objectives.

Motivation

The organizations with which we are concerned consist of varying numbers of individuals. A small business organization may be made up of as few as four or five individuals. In a major United States corporation, there may be more than a million individuals in the entire organization. How, then, do we ensure that the efforts of these individuals support the overall objectives of the total organization? That is one of the key questions that must be addressed and resolved with the effective implementation of a formal planning process.

The individuals in the formal organization must be motivated to achieve the objectives of the entire organization. Individuals look at their specific jobs, in many cases, not as an important piece of the overall fabric of organizational accomplishment but much more narrowly as ends in themselves, and many times not such important ends at that. With that type of construct in mind, it is relatively easy for individuals to rationalize that the attainment of their specific objectives is not important to the overall well being of the organization. They can easily rationalize failure or less than reasonable performance. The key to the successful implementation of a formal planning process is the ability to permeate the organization with meaningful objectives which are realistic and tied to the accomplishments of individuals.

The organization must harness the energy and capability of individuals, or it will not survive in the long run. The two concepts of organizational effectiveness and efficiency come into use here. Organizational effectiveness is concerned with whether or not the organization achieves its objectives. For example, an organization might have as its sole aim during a year the attainment of a net profit of $1 million. During the course of the year, the organization might have a variety of alternatives which it could pursue to achieve the goal. To be solely an effective organization, it could pursue any of those alternatives. However, the concept of organizational efficiency should always be considered. This concept examines the effectiveness of an organization but adds the dimension of an organization's maximizing its ends with minimal use of resources. Effectiveness is the extent to which an organization achieves its goals within the constraints of limited resources. An organization may be effective and not be efficient. An organization, to be effective, must achieve its ends. It does not have to achieve those ends efficiently. On the other hand, an organization may be efficient and not achieve its ends. In the latter case, the organization could be efficient and not be effective; and in the long run it may not survive in its environment. Although these two management concepts are relatively straightforward, the implications are not. How does an organization measure its effectiveness or efficiency? How should management direct an organization so that it will maximize its objectives while at the same time efficiently using its scarce resources? It is relatively simple to determine what we are trying to achieve but much more complex to set up systems and processes that will accomplish that measurement.

Short Range versus Long Range

One of the basic issues in any formal planning system is how to get operations personnel throughout the organization to take a little time away from the firefighting of today in order not to be consumed by the raging inferno of tomorrow. Time and again people say, "I just don't have time to plan." The truth of the matter is that the people who never have time to plan are the very ones that must take that precious time to operate more effectively in the future. The basic issue, then, becomes one of how an organization establishes a motivation or incentive system to induce the correct type of behavior from its managers and employees. How do you get a middle manager who in the next two weeks is expected to come up with some substantive increases in the period's sales figures to spend five hours on a very difficult strategic question that is currently being discussed for the five-year plan? How can you expect that manager to put the long-range strategic question into the proper perspective when compensation is made on the basis of the increase in this period's sales? The simple answer, proved time and again in the real world, is that you cannot. Sure, you will get the appropriate amount of lip service and faint support if the process is being supported up the line, but the dedication and commitment needed for survival of the operation are not there.

The basic question, then, is one of degree. If the organization really is sufficiently interested in long-term results, then it must change the compensation package accordingly. Too many firms, yes major firms in the United States today, still compensate for short-run performance while all the time talking about the benefits and vital necessity of long-range strategic planning. How is management supposed to react to these requirements when the so-called bottom line is almost always determined by short-run performance? So often we find that managers on the move stay in an organization only long enough to show good short-run operating results. They might say that to compensate on the basis of long-range goals would be counterproductive. One has to wonder. How many times have you seen actions taken that, in the short run, will reflect favorably on the division or department in which you are operating but which, if looked at from a long-run perspective, might have deleterious effects on the operation? Why does that occur? Why should that be allowed to continue? The answer is somewhat simplistic. It is just too hard! How do you provide an incentive for long-range performance when the person must be compensated month after month? It is much easier to use short-run profit maximization goals because we are involved with those easy-to-use accounting and financial statements that are so familiar to us. We do not have time (or do not take it) to go the next step and look at the real organizational meaning of these actions behind the short-term numbers. It is simply just too hard. Why should a company have to create an incentive for long-run behavior? The answer is simply that not all parts of an organization have the same needs. There are needs for short-term profitability, and there are needs for long-term technological development; and these are merely a small part of a long continuum. But the fact remains that we usually compensate the easy way. We motivate the behavior of the manager the easy way. It is not necessarily the most effective, efficient, or logical way, but certainly it is the easiest. In many respects, management is still more of an art than a science.

What do we do about this situation? Well, if we are really serious about the subject of long-range strategic planning, we must attempt to motivate the managers on more than a short-term objective basis in our organizations. The ground has been broken. It is not all unexplored territory, but it is relatively virgin. General Electric has found ways of motivating managers in the strategic planning system that they have developed. The GE system uses several terms to denote certain types of performance. For example, a unit (strategic business unit in their terminology) which should be maintained for the high cash flow that it provides to the balance of the corporation is called a "cow." The inference is that it should continue to be "milked" as much as it can in support of an overall corporate objective and as an integral part of the GE corporate strategy. GE has realized that the management of this "cow" should be compensated and that the specific incentive system used should be different from that of a high-technology company. If it is to optimize the long-run contribution to GE, a high-technology company must do much in the short term that will not necessarily lead to short-term profit maximization but that will provide the basis for long-term appreciation and contribution to GE. To put the right person in the right job has long been one of the fundamental jobs of top management. Executive selection and growth have a substantial effect on the long-run efficacy of the organization. Consequently, a manager in a job demanding entrepreneurial management efforts would receive different compensation and incentive programs than a manager in a job where he is expected to run the current operation as efficiently as possible in order to receive the maximum current return.

Compensation

GE has established incentive compensation based on three criteria: current financial results, future benefits, and other criteria. Before the SBU system was instituted, GE managers had been compensated on the basis of current earnings with an appropriate deduction for corporate services and capital. They found that since the units of the organization had to operate differently to optimize their particular contributions to the total organization, incentive compensation should be structured to motivate key managers. Units which were to be "milked" were heavily weighted on current financial performance while the portions of the business to be built up for the long run were weighted much less in the current financial performance category. On the other hand, cows were weighted very little on their future performance while the businesses of the future found incentive compensation packages heavily weighted toward future performance.

Conceptually, this appears to be an appropriate move. Key managers would be so motivated by their incentive compensation that their behavior would more closely coincide with the overall long-run objectives of the corporation. But are there any pitfalls? Yes, as in anything in which new ground is broken, there are bound to be some implementation problems. Probably the most difficult problem is measurement of the category called "future performance." If you are going to be using this category as an integral portion of a sophisticated compensation system, how will the measurement be made? That is a relevant question. Once we are forced to go beyond the current period financial results for a substantial portion of an executive compensation system, the problems become more difficult, but not insurmountable. The imagination and creativity of the individual must be exhibited here, and other measures of long-range performance must be found. There must be significant surrogates of future performance that would be meaningful in this situation. Future performance is not totally built on performance in a future period. Significant milestones must have been established and accomplished during the period of performance in question even though they may not have had a positive impact on current financial results. Key managers must be evaluated on the efficacy of their long-range strategy. They must have developed plans with which they will eventually provide major profits to the corporation. How are they doing in comparison to their plans? What were the critical facilities decisions on which the plan was based? What were the critical variables in the competitive environment analysis that showed the strategy was sound? How has the strategy which was approved several periods previously tracked during the current period? To be sure, these are more difficult questions to answer, and possibly they are a less finite system of measurement than the current-period profit and loss statement. But is that not what we are trying to do—motivate performance that may have been more difficult in the past because we want to exist as a viable organization in the future?

Strategic planning provides the technique to unify a corporation or an organization. Basic to this unifying concept is the thought of pervading and integrating. The personnel of the organization and the managers must know the game plan. They must have some feeling, tied into action plans at various levels, about how they contribute to the long-range organizational goals. Fundamental to this unifying force is the incentive compensation of key managers who must differentiate between old values like current financial performance and relatively new concepts (albeit difficult to implement) of trying to measure what will provide long-range performance. The concept of integration in a strategic planning system is a powerful one. But when executive compensation is tied to it, this power is magnified many times. We must learn to differentiate more and not subject all types of business and organizations to the same measurement devices. As we continually deal with scarce financial, physical, and personal resources, we must learn to use them more effectively and efficiently.

The effective strategic planning system must have incentives which will evoke behavior and performance required to support the objectives of the organization. Managers must strive to improve the incentive compensation system so that this behavior is in fact supportive and we do not continue to put a total premium on short-term financial performance to the detriment of the long-term organizational goals.

Performance Standards

In an effective planning system, standards must be set against which organizational performance is measured. The key is that the various parts of the organization must be measured against the correct standard. Short-term accomplishments must be used when, in the overall good of the organization, they count. When a longer-range posture must be taken, more long-range and potentially more difficult standards must be established.

Many times it is relatively easy to establish meaningful standards. In those cases, judgment must be used to ensure that the standards are appropriately set. However, in many instances, it is very difficult to set quantitative standards. Qualitative standards must be used, and are used successfully, in many instances, but an organization should endeavor to develop quantitative standards by which to measure performance. Standards play a vital role in establishing a yardstick for organizational performance to ensure that the output of the individuals and the groups meets the standard of performance required.

After standards are set, a key portion of the overall process is monitoring on a routinely scheduled basis. Results should be made available to management on variance from standards so that appropriate action can be taken. Appropriate action may mean that more resources must be applied to reach the standard or that the standard should be changed since it was incorrectly set.

Summary

Effective implementation of strategic planning is vital to an organization wanting to accrue its benefits. Integration of the organizational structure, the information system, the control system, the compensation system, and the planning system must be accomplished, or the organization will not l operating as efficiently as it should. The structure of the organizatioì should be determined by the strategy which the organization has developed. The strategic planning should be accomplished by line management in the organization and coordinated and assisted by staff personnel. Top management must be personally involved with and strongly support strategic planning in order to provide the extra emphasis needed to overcome the "brush fire" attitude that we sometimes are forced to follow. Implementation must be flexible so that the system can respond to its rapidly changing environment. Finally, resources and management attention must be accorded to the implementation phase of strategic planning since this may well be the most difficult and important part of the overall process.

Part II
An Application of
Strategic Planning

10 The Energy Environment from 1960 to 1975

The outlook for the United States energy industry depends mainly on its energy usage and the supply and demand of the components of that energy. This chapter will discuss these factors and the extant uncertainty in presenting the environment of the past fifteen years.

First, total United States and world energy production and consumption will be discussed. The various sectors of the energy industry will be analyzed for environmental trends. The exploration and production, distribution, marketing, and conversion sectors are subjected to different types and degrees of uncertainty. These uncertainties are discussed, and specific sources of uncertainty are listed. Finally, a summary will be presented, detailing the uncertainty in the energy industry.

Energy Analysis

Energy production and consumption can be discussed in terms of British thermal units Btu's). One Btu is the amount of heat required to raise the temperature of one pound of water one degree Fahrenheit. One Btu is a very small amount of energy. Btu equivalents are as follows:

1 barrel of crude oil	5.8 million Btu
1 cubic foot of natural gas	1032 Btu
1 ton of coal	25 million Btu (approximately)
1 kilowatthour of electricity	3.412 Btu

Total world energy production has increased by 4 1/2 percent compounded annually from 1960 through 1975 (Table 10-1). During that same period, coal production increased by 1 percent compounded annually, crude petroleum production increased by 7 percent compounded annually, natural gas production increased by 6 1/2 percent compounded annually, and hydro and nuclear production increased by 6 1/2 percent compounded annually.

Total world energy consumption also increased by 4 1/2 percent compounded annually from 1960 through 1975 (Table 10-2). Solid fuel consumption increased by 1 percent compounded annually from 1960 through 1975, as did both liquid fuel and natural gas consumption by 6 1/2 percent compounded annually, and hydro and nuclear electricity consumption by 6 1/4 percent compounded annually.

Total energy production in the United States alone increased by 4 percent compounded annually from 1960 through 1970, but decreased slightly from 1970 through 1975 (Table 10-3).

Total United States energy consumption has increased by 3 percent compounded annually from 1960 through 1975 (Table 10-4).

Electrical energy production in the 1940s and 1950s was based primarily upon coal utilization. However, it is now increasingly dependent upon natural gas and, to a lesser extent, nuclear power (Table 10-5). However, conversion efficiency declined by 4 percent during the period 1960 through 1975 (Table 10-6).

Table 10-1

Energy Production of the World, 1960 to 1975 (million metric tons of coal equivalent)

	1960	1965	1970	1975
World (total energy)	4297	5318	7386	8555
Coal	2191	2268	2397	2640
Crude Petroleum	1395	2001	3467	4035
Natural Gas	625	931	1367	1658
Hydro and Nuclear	86	117	154	221

Source: *Statistical Yearbook 1976,* United Nations, New York, 1977, page 48, Table 12; *Statistical Yearbook 1973,* 1974, page 48, Table 12; *Statistical Yearbook 1968,* 1969, p. 62, Table 12.

Table 10-2

Energy Consumption of the World, 1960 to 1975 (million metric tons of coal equivalent)

	1960	1965	1970	1975
World (total energy)	4233	5213	6834	8003
Solid Fuels	2204	2250	2399	2623
Liquid Fuels	1323	1919	2934	3526
Natural Gas	620[a]	926[a]	1346	1633
Hydro and Nuclear Electricity	86[a]	118[a]	154	221

Source: *Statistical Yearbook 1976,* United Nations New York, 1977, page 48, Table 12; *Statistical Yearbook 1973,* 1974, page 48, Table 12; *Statistical Yearbook 1968,* 1969, p. 62, Table 12.

[a]Includes imports.

Table 10-3
Energy Production in the United States, 1960 to 1975

	1960	1965	1970	1975[a]
Electrical energy production (trillion Btus)	41,553	49,074	62,481	60,103

Source: *Statistical Abstract of the United States: 1976*, p. 548, Table 904.
[a]Preliminary.

Table 10-4
Energy Consumption in the United States, 1960 to 1975

	1960	1965	1970	1975
Energy consumption (trillion Btus)	44,569	53,343	67,143	71,078

Source: *Statistical Abstract of the United States: 1976*, p. 549, Table 906.

Table 10-5
Percentage Distribution of the Type of Fuel for United States Electrical Energy Production, 1960 to 1975

	1960	1965	1970	1975
Coal	26.8%	27.3%	24.4%	25.8%
Oil	35.3	32.4	32.0	29.5
Natural Gas	34.0	36.0	38.9	36.9
Hydro	3.9	4.2	4.2	5.0
Nuclear	0.01	0.07	0.4	2.7

Source: *Statistical Abstract of the United States: 1976*, p. 548, Table 904.

Table 10-6
Conversion Efficiency in Converting Primary Fuels to Electrical Energy in the United States, 1960 to 1975

	1960	1965	1970	1975
Conversion efficiency	85.7%	85.0%	83.1%	81.0%

Source: *Statistical Abstract of the United States: 1976*, p. 549, Table 907.

Domestic production of crude oil increased 3 percent compounded annually from 1960 to 1970 and then dropped 13 percent by 1975 (Table 10-7). As domestic crude oil production was peaking, world production was increasing at 6 1/4 percent compounded annually from 1960 to 1975 (Table 10-8). Consequently, crude oil production outside the United States grew at almost 8 percent compounded annually from 1960 to 1975 (Table 10-9).

Total oil consumption in the United States increased at more than 3 1/2 percent compounded annually from 1960 to 1974 (Table 10-10). Oil consumption in the United States for electrical generation has increased 13 percent compounded annually from 1960 to 1974 (Table 10-11).

The United States portion of the total world crude oil production dropped from 33 percent in 1960 to 21 percent in 1970 and 16 percent (preliminary) in 1975 (Table 10-12). During the same period, imports rose at almost 3 percent compounded annually until 1970 and significantly increased 22 percent compounded annually to 1975.

Oil wells successfully completed from 1960 to 1970 declined by 41 percent and continued to decline through 1973 (Table 10-13). There was an increase of 35 percent in 1974.

Natural gas consumption increased at 5 percent compounded annually from 1960 to 1972 (Table 10-14). A decrease in this consumption by 11 percent appeared from 1973 to 1975.

However, domestic marketed gas production increased at less than 5 percent compounded annually until 1973 and actually decreased 11 percent by 1975 (Table 10-15).

Consequently, imports of natural gas increased at more than 14 percent compounded annually from 1960 to 1973, but decreased 7 percent from 1973 to 1975 (Table 10-16).

Table 10-7
Domestic Production of Crude Oil, 1960 to 1975

	1960	1965	1970	1975
Domestic crude oil production (million barrels)	2575	2849	3517	3057

Source: *Statistical Abstract of the United States: 1976*, p. 712, Table 1211.

Table 10-8
World Production of Crude Oil, 1960 to 1975

	1960	1965	1970	1975
World crude oil production (million barrels)	7689	11,058	16,719	19,655

Source: *Statistical Abstract of the United States: 1976*, p. 712, Table 1211.

Table 10-9
World Production of Crude Oil outside the United States, 1960 to 1975

	1960	1965	1970	1975
World less U.S. crude oil production (million barrels)	5114	8209	13,202	16,598

Source: *Statistical Abstract of the United States: 1976*, p. 712, Table 1211.

Table 10-10
Total Domestic Consumption of Petroleum, 1960 to 1974

	1960	1965	1970	1974[a]
Total oil consumption (million barrels)	3611	4202	5365	6078

Source: *Statistical Abstract of the United States: 1976*, p. 711, Table 1210.
[a]Preliminary.

Table 10-11
Oil Consumption in the United States for Electrical Generation, 1960 to 1974

	1960	1965	1970	1974[a]
Oil consumption for electical generation (million barrels)	90	119	334	560

Source: *Statistical Abstract of the United States: 1976*, p. 711, Table 1210.
[a]Preliminary.

Table 10-12
Imports of Crude Oil to the United States, 1960 to 1975

	1960	1965	1970	1975[a]
U.S. crude oil imports (million barrels)	372	452	483	1498

Source: *Statistical Abstract of the United States: 1976*, p. 712, Table 1211.
[a]Preliminary.

Table 10-13
Oil Wells Successfully Completed in the United States, 1960 to 1974

	1960	1965	1970	1973	1974
Oil wells successfully completed	21,294	18,857	12,547	9705	13,073

Source: *Statistical Abstract of the United States: 1976*, p. 713, Table 1214.

Table 10-14

Natural Gas Consumption in the United States, 1960 to 1975

	1960	1965	1970	1972	1975
Natural gas consumption (billion cubic feet)	12,509	16,033	22,046	23,009	20,410

Source: *Statistical Abstract of the United States: 1976,* p. 715, Table 1217.

Table 10-15

United States Natural Gas Marketed Production, 1960 to 1975

	1960	1965	1970	1973	1975
Natural gas marketed production (billion cubic feet)	12,771	16,040	21,921	22,647	20,109

Source: *Statistical Abstract of the United States: 1976,* p. 715, Table 1217.

Table 10-16

United States Natural Gas Imports, 1960 to 1975

	1960	1965	1970	1973	1975
Natural gas imports (billion cubic feet)	156	456	821	1033	953

Source: *Statistical Abstract of the United States: 1976,* p. 715, Table 1217.

Proved reserves of natural gas increased at 1 percent compounded annually from 1960 to 1970 and then decreased 22 percent by 1975 (Table 10-17).

Natural gas consumption in the United States for electrical generation (utilities) increased at 7 percent compounded annually from 1960 to 1971 (Table 10-18). Then from 1972 to 1975 this consumption decreased by 21 percent.

Coal production in the United States increased at 3 percent compounded annually from 1960 to 1970 and then declined 2 percent from 1970 to 1973 (Table 10-19). An increase occurred again from 1973 to 1975 by almost 4 percent, compounded annually.

Coal consumption in the United States increased at more than 2 percent compounded annually from 1960 to 1973 and then declined slightly in 1974 (Table 10-20).

While overall coal consumption was increasing 2 percent compounded annually from 1960 to 1974, coal consumption for electrical generation was increasing more than 5 percent compounded annually (Table 10-21).

Table 10-17
Proved Reserves of Natural Gas in the United States, 1960 to 1975

	1960	1965	1970	1975
Proved natural gas reserves (trillion cubic feet)	264	286	291	228

Source: *Statistical Abstract of the United States: 1976*, p. 715, Table 1217.

Table 10-18
Natural Gas Consumption in the United States for Electrical Generation, 1960 to 1975

	1960	1965	1970	1971	1975
Natural gas consumption for electrical generation (billion cubic feet)	1725	2318	3894	3993	3147

Source: *Statistical Abstract of the United States: 1976*, p. 715, Table 1217.

Table 10-19
Total Coal Production in the United States, 1960 to 1975

	1960	1965	1970	1973	1975[a]
Coal production (million short tons)	434	527	613	599	646

Source: *Statistical Abstract of the United States: 1976*, p. 710, Table 1207.
[a]Preliminary.

Table 10-20
Total Coal Consumption in the United States, 1960 to 1974

	1960	1965	1970	1973	1974[a]
Coal consumption (million short tons)	398	472	524	562	558

Source: *Statistical Abstract of the United States: 1976*, p. 711, Table 1210.
[a]Preliminary.

Table 10-21
Coal Consumption for Electrical Generation, 1960 to 1974

	1960	1965	1970	1974[a]
Coal consumption for electrical generation (million short tons)	177	245	321	392

Source: *Statistical Abstract of the United States: 1976*, p. 711, Table 1210.
[a]Preliminary.

Nuclear power plant capacity in the United States has increased more than 30 percent compounded annually from 1960 to 1975 (Table 10-22). As the nuclear power plant capacity has increased from 1960 to 1975 on an absolute scale, it has increased from 0.2 to 8.3 percent of the total electric utility capacity (Table 10-23). Nuclear capacity ordered from manufacturers has increased initially even more sharply, at more than 50 percent compounded on an annual rate from 1960 to 1974, with a sharp 88 percent decrease in 1975.

Energy Industry Uncertainty

The primary types of uncertainty facing companies in the energy industry are economic, technological, political, environmental, and social. Uncertainty is defined in Webster's as doubt, not surely known, questionable, or problematical. Decision makers must deal with information that may be uncertain or estimated. Economic uncertainty refers to relationships of an organization in economic or monetary terms and the consequences of its actions measured in such terms as income, expenditures, return on investment, and other economic measures. Technological uncertainty refers to relationships of technical progress in the use of machinery in industry. Political uncertainty is concerned with the government or state and the reliability of information or action associated with federal, state, and local governments. Environmental uncertainty involves relationships of organizations in the energy industry and its physical or living environment and the impact of an organization on its physical environment. Social uncertainty refers to relationships with human beings and the impact of an organization on the personal situation.

Production Sector

Several disturbing trends in the production sector of the petroleum industry were evident in the 1960s. These trends contributed to the economic uncertainty in the production sector. First, the relative success of United States exploratory drilling was declining, continuing a long-term trend. Success in drilling new-field wildcat wells dropped from 10.18 to 8.49 percent from 1960 to 1968 (Table 10-24). However, in the 1970s the trend was dramatically reversed. The success in drilling all exploratory wells dropped from 18.70 to 14.56 percent from 1960 to 1968 and then was dramatically reversed in the 1970s (Table 10-25).

Second, a downward trend in the number of drilling rigs in the United States continued during the 1960s. The number of rigs peaked in the early

Table 10-22
Nuclear Power Plant Capacity in the United States, 1960 to 1975

	1960	1965	1970	1975
Nuclear power plant capacity (megawatts)	381	1027	7498	39,595

Source: *Statistical Abstract of the United States: 1976*, p. 563, Table 934.

Table 10-23
Nuclear Capacity Ordered from Manufacturers, 1960 to 1975

	1960	1965	1970	1974	1975
Nuclear capacity ordered (megawatts)	17	4441	14,272	35,631	4100

Source: *Statistical Abstract of the United States: 1976*, p. 563, Table 934.

Table 10-24
Relative Success of New-Field Wildcat Exploratory Drilling, 1960 to 1975

	1960	1965	1970	1975
Successful new-field wildcat wells	10.2%	10.3%	9.7%	14.4%

Source: *Twentieth Century Petroleum Statistics: 1976*, De Golyer and MacNaughton, Dallas, Texas, p. 36.

Table 10-25
Relative Success of All Exploratory Drilling, 1960 to 1975

	1960	1965	1970	1975
Successful exploratory wells	18.7%	15.4%	16.5%	23.3%

Source: *Twentieth Century Petroleum Statistics: 1976*, De Golyer and MacNaughton, Dallas, Texas, p. 36.

1950s and continually declined until a slight increase was realized in the early 1970s (Table 10-26). The use of drilling rigs declined more than 8 percent from 1968 to 1972 and then steadily increased 43 percent through 1976.

Third, natural gas availability in the future in required quantities is very questionable. Although the estimated annual discovery of natural gas reserves in the United States averaged 12 trillion cubic feet from 1920 to 1960, the average from 1961 to 1969 was 7.6 trillion cubic feet and the annual total for 1969 decreased 85 percent below that of 1960 (Table 10-27).

Fourth, exposure to economic uncertainty in the world market is greater than in the United States market (Table 10-28).

Fifth, substantial initial investments are required for exploration and production rights with substantial economic uncertainty.

Table 10-26
Active Drilling Rigs in the United States, 1968 to 1976

	1968	1972	1976
Drilling rigs in use	1508	1381	1979

Source: *Basic Petroleum Data Book,* American Petroleum Institute, Washington, D.C., 1975 edition, section III, Table 15.

Table 10-27
Estimated Annual Discoveries of Natural Gas Reserves in the United States, 1920 to 1969

	1920-1960 Average	1960	1964	1969
Estimated discoveries of natural gas reserves (billions cubic feet)	12	13.6	9.0	2.1

Source: *Petroleum Facts and Figures,* American Petroleum Institute, Washington, D.C., 1971 edition, p. 117.

Table 10-28
Consumer Price Index of Selected Countries of the World, 1965 to 1975

	1965	1973	1975
Australia	86	123	163
Israel	82	152	295
Japan	77	124	172
New Zealand	79	128	163
Philippines	82	153	235
South Africa	85	124	157
Syrian Arab Republic	85	127	170
United States (1970 = 100)	81	114	139

Source: *Statistical Yearbook 1976,* United Nations, New York, 1974, p. 631, Table 181.

The North Slope oil discovery in Alaska provided more needed crude reserves for the United States, but it required large investments. The major discovery in the North Sea provided vast potential benefits, but also included substantial economic uncertainty.

Several trends in the industry contributed to technological uncertainty. First, United States wells, both exploratory and producing, are becoming deeper and more expensive. Exploratory deep wells (15,000 feet and below) completed increased by 12 percent from 1960 to 1968 (Table 10-29). Producing deep wells completed increased by 43 percent from 1960 to 1968

(Table 10-30). Total footage drilled in deep wells increased 80 percent from 1960 to 1968 (Table 10-31). The average deep-well depth increased 7 percent from 1960 to 1968 (Table 10-32).

The deepest producing well continued a long-term trend and increased 10 percent from 1960 to 1968 (Table 10-33). The average deep-well cost increased 3 percent compounded annually from 1960 to 1968 (Table 10-34). The average cost per foot increased 2 percent compounded annually from 1960 to 1968 (Table 10-35).

Second, United States crude oil reserves were declining. Reserves discovered in new fields declined 32 percent from 1960 to 1969 (Table 10-36).

Reserves discovered in new pools in old fields increased significantly in the early 1960s and then declined, yet showed an overall increase of 3 percent compounded annually from 1960 to 1969 (Table 10-37). Crude oil proved reserves during the period decreased more than 6 percent (Table 10-38).

Substantial political uncertainty was evident in the production sector. First, the stability of the governing unit and the contract with the governing unit contribute to the uncertainty in the production sector. Second, the relative stability of the currency and money-market rates is less in the production sector of the industry (Tables 10-39 and 10-40).

Third, the stability of the tax rate and type of tax has a pronounced effect on the production sector. Fourth, the stability of returns has a pronounced effect on the uncertainty in the production sector.

Table 10-29
Exploratory Deep Wells Completed in the United States, 1960 to 1968

	1960	1964	1968
Exploratory deep wells completed	134	141	150

Source: *Petroleum Facts and Figures,* American Petroleum Institute, Washington, D.C., 1971 edition, p. 37.

Table 10-30
Producing Deep Wells Completed in the United States, 1960 to 1968

	1960	1964	1968
Producing deep wells completed	136	150	194

Source: *Petroleum Facts and Figures,* American Petroleum Institute, Washington, D.C., 1971 edition, p. 37.

Table 10-31

Total Footage Drilled in Deep Wells in the United States, 1960 to 1968 (millions)

	1960	1964	1968
Total footage drilled	3.859	5.116	6.931

Source: *Petroleum Facts and Figures,* American Petroleum Institute, Washington, D.C., 1971 edition, p. 37.

Table 10-32

Average Deep-Well Depth in the United States, 1960 to 1968

	1960	1964	1968
Average deep well depth (feet)	15,945	16,610	17,072

Source: *Petroleum Facts and Figures,* American Petroleum Institute, Washington, D.C., 1971 edition, p. 37.

Table 10-33

Deepest Producing Well in the United States, 1960 to 1968

	1960	1964	1968
Deepest producing well (feet)	20,745	21,793	22,790

Source: *Petroleum Facts and Figures,* American Petroleum Institute, Washington, D.C., 1971 edition, p. 37.

Table 10-34

Average Deep-Well Cost in the United States, 1960 to 1968

	1960	1964	1968
Average deep-well cost	$675,000	$653,256	$899,991

Source: *Petroleum Facts and Figures,* American Petroleum Institute, Washington, D.C., 1971 edition, p. 37.

Table 10-35

Average Cost per Foot of Deep Wells Drilled in the United States, 1960 to 1968

	1960	1964	1968
Average cost per foot	$42.50	$39.33	$52.13

Source: *Petroleum Facts and Figures,* American Petroleum Institute, Washington, D.C., 1971 edition, p. 37.

Table 10-36
Crude Oil Reserves Discovered in New Fields in the United States, 1960 to 1969

	1960	*1964*	*1969*
Reserves discovered in new fields (thousand barrels)	141,296	126,682	96,435

Source: *Petroleum Facts and Figures,* American Petroleum Institute, Washington, D.C., 1971 edition, p. 110.

Table 10-37
Reserves Discovered in New Pools in Old Fields in the United States, 1960 to 1969

	1960	*1964*	*1969*
Reserves discovered in new pools in old fields (thousand barrels)	112,560	219,611	150,749

Source: *Petroleum Facts and Figures,* American Petroleum Institute, Washington, D.C., 1971 edition, p. 110.

Table 10-38
Crude Oil Proved Reserves in the United States, 1960 to 1969

	1960	*1964*	*1969*
Crude oil proved reserves (thousand barrels)	31,613,211	30,990,518	29,631,862

Source: *Petroleum Facts and Figures,* American Petroleum Institute, Washington, D.C., 1971 edition, p. 110.

Table 10-39
Exchange Rates of Selected Countries, 1969 to 1975 (national currency per U.S. dollar)

	1969	*1971*	*1973*	*1975*
Algeria (Dinar)	4.937	4.644	4.185	4.125
Australia (Dollar)	0.8945	0.8396	0.6720	0.7955
Canada (Dollar)	1.0728	1.0022	0.9958	1.0164
Ethiopia (Dollar)	2.50	2.52	2.09	2.09
India[a] (Rupee)	7.492	7.214	8.130	8.937
Japan (Yen)	357.8	314.8	280.0	305.2
Nigeria (Naira)	0.3571	0.3289	0.6579	0.6267

Source: *Statistical Yearbook 1976,* United Nations, New York, 1977, p. 695, Table 192.
[a]Selling rate.

Table 10-40
Money-Market Rates of Selected Countries, 1969 to 1975

		1969	1971	1973	1975
Canada	(A)	7.19	3.56	5.47	7.40
India	(B)	3.91	5.83	5.50	–
Japan	(B)	7.70	6.42	7.16	10.67
South Africa	(A)	4.61	5.38	3.18	6.12
U.S.	(A)	6.69	4.34	7.03	5.82

Source: *Statistical Yearbook 1976,* United Nations, New York, 1977, p. 717, Table 196.
(A) Treasury bill rate.
(B) Call money rate.
(percent per annum)

Substantial environmental uncertainty was evident in the production sector of the energy industry. First, substantial uncertainty resulted from the instability of various production techniques. Second, there is substantial risk in the production sector in the development of new secondary and tertiary recovery methods.

Third, substantial uncertainty exists because of the problems involved in bringing substantial quantities of foreign oil to the United States with no existing supertanker ports.

Fourth, the stability of the OPEC nations creates substantial uncertainty in the production sector.

Substantial social uncertainty was evident in the production sector of the energy industry. First, the population and the birthrate are much more uncertain in foreign countries than in the United States (Table 10-41).

Second, the rest of the world outside the United States is subject to greater relative shifts in economic conditions.

Distribution Sector

The distribution sector shows the same general growth characteristics exhibited by the other sectors in the energy continuum. Increases were evident in total petroleum pipeline mileage, utility gas mains, and pipeline receipts of crude oil and refined products.

Total petroleum pipeline mileage increased at 1 percent compounded annually from 1962 to 1974 (Table 10-42). The miles of all utility gas mains increased at more than 3 percent compounded annually from 1962 to 1974 (Table 10-43). However, the miles of natural gas mains increased at more than 4 percent compounded annually from 1960 to 1968 (Table 10-44).

Table 10-41
Population of Selected Countries, 1963 to 1975 (millions)

	1963	1970	1972	1975	Annual Rate of Increase
Algeria	11.2	14.3	15.3	16.8	3.2
Egypt	27.9	33.3	34.9	37.2	2.2
Nigeria	41.3	55.1	58.2	62.9	2.7
South Africa	18.1	22.5	23.0	25.5	2.5
Hong Kong	3.4	4.0	4.1	4.4	2.0
India	462.0	539.1	563.5	598.1	2.1
Iraq	7.6	9.4	10.1	11.1	3.3
Israel	2.4	2.9	3.1	3.4	3.1
Australia	11.0	12.5	13.0	13.5	1.5
U.S.	189.2	204.9	208.8	213.6	0.8

Source: *Statistical Yearbook 1976,* United Nations, New York, 1977, p. 68, Table 18.

Table 10-42
Total Petroleum Pipeline Mileage in the United States, 1962 to 1974

	1962	1968	1974
Petroleum pipeline mileage	200,543	209,478	222,355

Source: *Basic Petroleum Data Book,,* American Petroleum Institute, Washington, D.C., 1975 edition, section XII, Table I.

Table 10-43
Miles of Utility Gas Main in the United States, 1962 to 1974

	1962	1968	1974
Utility gas main (thousands)	428.1	562.7	645.6

Source: *Basic Petroleum Data Book,* American Petroleum Institute, Washington, D.C., 1975 edition, section XII, Table 2.

Table 10-44
Miles of Utility Natural Gas Mains in the United States, 1960 to 1968

	1960	1964	1968
Natural gas mains	607,980	774,510	852,420

Source: *Petroleum Facts and Figures,* American Petroleum Institute, Washington, D.C., 1971 edition, pp. 226, 228, 230.

Pipeline receipts of crude oil and refined products increased 5 percent compounded annually from 1960 to 1968 (Table 10-45).

United States refinery capacity reflected a mixed picture. The total number of refineries declined by 8 percent from 1960 to 1971, then increased by 1 percent by 1975 (Table 10-46).

However, the daily average crude oil capacity increased 3 percent compounded annually from 1960 to 1975 (Table 10-47).

Total United States refinery input during the 1960s followed a long-term trend of increasing input of both domestic and foreign crude. Domestic crude input increased at 3 percent compounded annually from 1960 to 1970 and actually decreased 12 percent by 1975 (Table 10-48). During this same period foreign crude steadily increased more than 9 percent compounded annually from 1960 to 1975.

The 1960s also reflected the major changes taking place in the world tanker fleet. Tankers under 50,000 dwt accounted for more than 96 percent

Table 10-45
Pipeline Receipts of Crude Oil and Refined Product in the United States, 1960 to 1968

	1960	1964	1968
Pipeline receipts of crude oil and refined product (billion barrels)	4.783	5.576	7.289

Source: *Petroleum Facts and Figures*, American Petroleum Institute, Washington, D.C., 1971 edition, p. 241.

Table 10-46
Total Number of Refineries in the United States, 1960 to 1975

	1960	1965	1970	1975[a]
Total refineries	311	286	279	290

Source: *Statistical Abstract of the United States: 1976*, p. 712, Table 1211.
[a]Preliminary.

Table 10-47
Daily Crude Oil Capacity in the United States, 1960 to 1975

	1960	1965	1970	1975[a]
Crude oil capacity (million barrels per day)	10.0	10.5	13.0	15.2

Source: *Statistical Abstract of the United States: 1976*, p. 712, Table 1211.
[a]Preliminary.

of the total world tanker capacity in 1960; by 1969 this figure had dropped to less than 45 percent (Table 10-49). Large tankers over 110,000 dwt had increased from zero in 1960 to 17.3 percent of the world capacity in 1969.

The United States tanker fleet increased 3.8 percent measured in dwt from 1960 to 1972 while the United States tanker fleet as a percentage of the world's total capacity dropped from 14.1 percent to less than 6 percent during the same period.

The distribution sector of the energy industry evidenced sources of uncertainty somewhat different from those of the production sector. Economic uncertainties in the production sector (Tables 10-24 through 10-28) were different for the distribution sector. The uncertainty provided by the declining effectiveness of exploratory drilling was reduced on the distribution sector. Additionally, the large reduction in estimated natural gas annual discoveries had much less impact on the distribution sector.

The distribution sector is also subject to less economic uncertainty because of its reduced exposure to the economics of fewer foreign countries. This affects not only the stability of raw material input and output but also the economic uncertainty of offshore drilling. Substantial uncertainty is ex-

Table 10-48
United States Refinery Input of Domestic and Foreign Crude, 1960 to 1975 (million barrels)

	1960	1965	1970	1972	1975[a]
Domestic crude	2582	2848	3485	3474	3047
Foreign crude	371	453	482	807	1494

Source: *Statistical Abstract of the United States: 1976*, p. 712, Table 1212.

Table 10-49
World Tanker Carrying Capacity by Size of Vessel, 1960 to 1969

	1960	1964	1969
Under 16,999 dwt	30.5%	16.5%	7.1%
17,000 - 29,999 dwt	35.7	29.5	17.8
30,000 - 49,999 dwt	30.4	33.6	19.9
50,000 - 74,999 dwt	2.2	14.5	18.6
75,000 - 109,999 dwt	1.2	5.5	19.2
110,000 dwt and over	−	0.4	17.3

Source: *Petroleum Facts and Figures*, American Petroleum Institute, Washington, D.C., 1971 edition, p. 247.

tant in the distribution problems of the North Slope and the North Sea, but they are relatively small compared to the exploration and production problems involved.

Technological uncertainty in the distribution sector is also less than that in the production sector. As United States wells, both exploratory and producing, are becoming deeper and more expensive (Tables 10-29 to 10-35), the primary impact is on the production sector. As the discovery of new fields of crude oil decreased (Table 10-36), less technological uncertainty is extant in the distribution sector. As reserves in new pools in old fields increased slightly (Table 10-37) and proved crude oil reserves declined (Table 10-38), there was a significant lessening of uncertainty in the distribution sector in contrast to the production sector.

The political uncertainty extant in the distribution sector is significant but less than that in the production sector. Risk involved in the stability of the governing unit is present but is less than that in the production sector because of the size of the relative investments involved. The stability of the currency and money-market rates (Tables 10-39 and 10-40) creates less uncertainty in the distribution sector due to less exposure than in the production sector. The stability of tax rates and type of taxes provides uncertainty in the distribution sector, but again it is less than in the production sector because the exposure of the distribution sector is more limited. The stability of return is also less on the distribution sector because of the reduced exposure to the risk than on the production sector.

The environmental uncertainty extant in the distribution sector is much less than that in the production sector. The uncertainty of new emergency technologies on the environment is limited in the distribution sector. The effect of production methods on the distribution sector is also substantially reduced. The stability of the OPEC nations produces less environmental uncertainty because of the limited exposure in the distribution sector. However, there is substantial uncertainty resulting from the absence of supertanker ports in the United States.

There is a substantial amount of social uncertainty in the distribution sector because of the exposure to foreign population growth and economic trends (Table 10-41). However, the uncertainty is less than in the production sector owing to the lower exposure.

Marketing Sector

Marketing demand for petroleum products continued to grow during the 1960s. Demand for crude oil products varies widely. While demand for gasoline and distillate fuel oil increased by 3 percent compounded annually, demand for jet fuel increased more than 9 percent compounded annually from 1960 to 1973 (Table 10-50). Then a slight decrease was evidenced in these areas by 1975.

Service stations showed increased dollar sales during the 1960s, continuing a long-term trend. In addition, the number of service stations continued a long-term growth trend. Total dollar sales volume of service stations in the United States increased more than 5 percent compounded annually from 1960 to 1972 (Table 10-51). The total number of service stations in the United States increased at less than 1 percent compounded annually from 1960 to 1972 (Table 10-52). Service stations sales as a percentage of total retail sales peaked in 1961 and then steadily declined (Table 10-53).

The marketing sector of the energy industry evidenced different sources of uncertainty from the production and distribution sectors. Economic uncertainty in the production sector (Tables 10-24 through 10-28) was different for the marketing sector. The uncertainty created by the declining effectiveness of exploratory drilling was minimal on the marketing sector, as was the large reduction in estimated natural gas annual discoveries.

The marketing sector is also subject to less economic uncertainty because of its minimal exposure to the economics of foreign countries. This affects not only the stability of raw material input and output but also the economic uncertainty of offshore drilling. The economic uncertainty of North Slope and North Sea oil in the marketing sector is minimal relative to that in the production and distribution sectors.

Technological uncertainty in the marketing sector is also less than that in the production and distribution sectors. As United States wells, both exploratory and producing, are becoming deeper and more expensive (Tables 10-29 to 10-35), increased market prices will be set. Since crude oil discoveries in new fields have decreased (Table 10-36), minimal uncertainty is extant in the marketing sector. Even though reserves in new pools in old fields increased slightly (Table 10-37) and crude oil proved reserves declined (Table 10-38), minimal impact is still extant in the marketing sector.

Political uncertainty is present in the marketing sector but substantially less than in the production and distribution sectors. The primary reason is

Table 10-50
Demand for Selected Crude Oil Products, 1960 to 1975 (million barrels)

	1960	1965	1970	1973	1975[a]
Demand for gasoline	1510	1694	2100	2399	2393
Demand for distillate oil	667	765	896	1029	968
Demand for jet fuel	88	191	302	314	318

Source: *Statistical Abstract of the United States: 1976*, p. 712, Table 1212.
[a]Preliminary.

Table 10-51
Total Retail Sales of United States Service Stations, 1960 to 1972

	1960	1967	1972
Service stations retail sales (billions)	$17,594	$22,709	$33,655

Source: *Statistical Abstract of the United States: 1976,* p. 592, Table 987.

Table 10-52
Total United States Service Stations, 1960 to 1972

	1960	1967	1972
Total service stations	208,750	213,100	226,500

Source: *Statistical Abstract of the United States: 1976,* p. 592, Table 987.

Table 10-53
Service Station Sales as a Percentage of Total Retail Sales, 1960 to 1968

	1960	1961	1964	1968
Service station sales as a percentage of total retail sales	8.01	8.21	7.75	7.22

Source: *Petroleum Facts and Figures,* American Petroleum Institute, Washington, D.C., 1971 edition, p. 301.

that the marketing sector is subject solely to the governing unit of the United States as opposed to the substantial foreign exposure of the production sector and the significant foreign exposure of the distribution sector. The stability of the currency and money-market rates (Tables 10-39 and 10-40) is greater owing to exclusive United States exposure. The stability of the banking system and stability of return are more certain in the marketing sector than in the production and distribution sectors owing to exposure solely to the United States system.

Environmental uncertainty extant in the marketing sector is much less than that in the production and distribution sectors. The uncertainty of new, emerging energy technology is minimal or zero in the marketing sector. The stability of the OPEC nations produces little uncertainty owing to the limited downstream exposure of the marketing sector. There is little uncertainty because of the absence of supertanker ports in the United States.

There is substantially less social uncertainty in the marketing sector because its exposure is limited to the United States population and economic status trends. Foreign exposure in the production and distribution sectors contributes substantially to the uncertainty in those sectors.

Conversion Sector

The conversion sector of the energy industry has less uncertainty than the preceding sectors. Economic uncertainty in the production sector (Tables 10-24 through 10-28) was minimal for the conversion sector. Uncertainty created by declining effectiveness of exploratory drilling and a large reduction in estimated natural gas annual discoveries is minimized by the ability of the conversion sector to pass on increased fuel costs to its customers. Any potential uncertainty for the conversion sector resulting from foreign exposure, such as stability of raw material input and output, is also ameliorated by the economic realities of the market base. Uncertainties caused by difficulties in determining initial product cost and production cost and sustaining economic delivery rates in the production sector are nonexistent in the conversion sector.

Stability of competition is the most substantial source of uncertainty in the preceding energy industry sectors. However, the conversion sector has a very stable competitive structure. Availability of North Slope and North Sea oil causes minimal uncertainty in this sector.

The size of investment to ensure product supply is potentially a substantial source of uncertainty in the conversion sector owing to the magnitude of the capital investment required. However, due to the relatively small economic risk encountered by companies in this sector and the relatively stable competition, the size of investment is not a substantial source of uncertainty.

Investments for offshore leases and offshore drilling normally create little uncertainty in the conversion sector. Also, little uncertainty is evident in the stability of product sources. Stability of demand for product may provide the most substantial economic uncertainty of all the economic factors. Prior to the energy crisis, this factor would have provided minimal uncertainty because product demand was relatively stable. However, more uncertainty exists now as a result of the reduction of product demand because of increased cost and conservation efforts in the United States.

Technological uncertainty in the conversion sector is minimal. The sources of uncertainty for the preceding parts of the energy continuum are basically irrelevant to the conversion sector. One source of uncertainty is the present move to more nuclear power generating plants, but the technology for this evolution is available in sufficient depth and at reasonable enough cost to minimize the uncertainty associated with it.

Political uncertainty extant in the conversion sector is substantially minimized owing to the exposure to United States governing units only. Although conversion-sector companies may be directly tied to political agreements, this potential source of uncertainty is ameliorated as a result of its United States exposure.

There is some environmental uncertainty extant in the conversion sector. The uncertainty of emerging technologies is limited here, as is the stability of OPEC nations and accepting substantial quantities of foreign oil. However, the conversion sector experiences substantial environmental uncertainty in the construction of new generating plants, because of recent legislation and public awareness of environmental concerns.

There is substantially less social uncertainty in the conversion sector because exposure is limited to United States population and economic trends.

Summary

This chapter has described the energy environment from 1960 to 1975. Specific sources of uncertainty in the various sectors of the energy industry have been discussed. The discussion which established the more substantial uncertainty at the production end of the continuum, with the uncertainty diminishing toward the conversion sector, is summarized in Appendix 10A.

**Appendix 10A:
Matrixes of Uncertainty
in the Energy Industry**

Table 10A-1
Economic Uncertainty in the Energy Industry

Economic Uncertainties	Production Sector	Distribution Sector	Marketing Sector	Conversion Sector
Stability of raw material input—physical	Continual risk associated with oil exploration	Limited risk of change in oil refining areas and ocean transport	Little risk of basic change	Little risk of basic change
Stability of raw material input—price	Exposure to risk on world market greater than on U.S. market only	Limited risk of change in oil refining areas and ocean transport	Little risk of basic change	Little risk of basic change
Stability of output—physical	Continual risk because of high exploration risk	Limited risk of change in oil refining areas and ocean transport	Little risk of basic change	Little risk of basic change
Stability of output—price	Exposure to risk on world market greater than on U.S. market only	Limited risk of change in oil refining areas and ocean transport	Little risk of basic change	Little risk of basic change
Difficulty in finding product	Continual risk associated with oil exploration	Limited risk of change in oil refining areas and ocean transport	Little risk of basic change	Little risk of basic change
Difficulty in determining size of production discovery	Continual risk associated with oil exploration	Not applicable	Not applicable	Not applicable
Difficulty in determining initial product cost	Continual risk associated with oil exploration	Not applicable	Not applicable	Not applicable
Difficulty in determining production cost	Continual risk associated with oil exploration	Not applicable	Not applicable	Not applicable
Difficulty in sustaining economic delivery rate	Continual risk associated with oil exploration	Not applicable	Not applicable	Not applicable
Stability of competition	Continual risk of change of competition	Continual risk of change of competition	Limited risk of change in competition	Little risk of basic change

Table 10A-1 (cont.)

Economic Uncertainties	Production Sector	Distribution Sector	Marketing Sector	Conversion Sector
Availability of North Slope Oil	Continual risk because of size/scope of investment	Substantial risk owing to required investment in distribution system and ocean transport	Little risk of basic change	Little risk of basic change
Availability of North Sea Oil	Continual risk because of size/scope of investment	Substantial risk owing to required investment in distribution system	Little risk of basic change	Little risk of basic change
Size of investment required to ensure product supply	Exposure to substantial investment risk	Exposure to limited investment risk	Little risk of basic change	Little risk of basic change
Size of investment to get offshore leases	Exposure to substantial investment risk	Exposure to limited investment risk	Little risk of basic change	Little risk of basic change
Size of investment to drill offshore	Exposure to substantial investment risk	Exposure to limited investment risk	Little risk of basic change	Little risk of basic change
Stability of product sources	Continual risk associated with declining product sources	Limited risk of change in oil refining and ocean transport areas	Little risk of basic change	Little risk of basic change
Stability of demand for product	Limited risk	Limited risk in oil refining and ocean transport	Little risk of basic change	Little risk of basic change

Table 10A-2
Technological Uncertainty in the Energy Industry

Technological Uncertainties	Production Sector	Distribution Sector	Marketing Sector	Conversion Sector
Product cost	Foreign and U.S.	Foreign and U.S.	U.S. only	U.S. only
Total footage drilled in deep wells	Increasing risk owing to depth of drilling	Limited risk in oil refining and ocean transportation	Little risk of basic change	Little risk of basic change
Average deep-well depth	Increasing risk owing to depth of drilling	Limited risk in oil refining and ocean transportation	Little risk of basic change	Little risk of basic change
Deepest producing well	Increasing risk owing to depth of drilling	Limited risk in oil refining and ocean transportation	Little risk of basic change	Little risk of basic change
Average deep-well cost	Increasing risk owing to cost of drilling	Limited risk in oil refining and ocean transportation	Little risk of basic change	Little risk of basic change
Average cost per foot of deep wells	Increasing risk owing to cost of drilling	Limited risk in oil refining and ocean transportation	Little risk of basic change	Little risk of basic change
Crude oil reserves discovered in new fields	Increasing risk owing to increased reliance on old fields	Limited risk in oil refining and ocean transportation	Little risk of basic change	Little risk of basic change
Crude oil reserves discovered in new pool in old fields	Increasing risk owing to increased reliance on old fields	Limited risk in oil refining and ocean transportation	Little risk of basic change	Little risk of basic change
Reduction in total crude reserves	Increasing risk owing to reliance on crude oil	Limited risk in oil refining and ocean transportation	Little risk of basic change	Little risk of basic change

Table 10A-3
Political Uncertainty in the Energy Industry

Political Uncertainties	Production Sector	Distribution Sector	Marketing Sector	Conversion Sector
Governing unit	Foreign and U.S.	Foreign and U.S.	U.S. only	U.S. only
Stability of governing unit	Continual risk of change in government in oil production areas	Limited risk of change in oil refining areas; not applicable to ocean transport	Little risk of basic change	Little risk of basic change
Stability of contract with governing unit	Continual risk of unilateral change in charter in oil production areas	Limited risk of unilateral change in charter in oil refining areas; not applicable to ocean transport	Little risk of basic change	Little risk of basic change
Stability of currency	Continual risk of currency revaluation	Limited risk of currency revaluation	Not applicable	Not applicable
Stability of price level	Exposure to foreign inflation, often greater than U.S.	Exposure to foreign inflation, often greater than U.S.	Exposure to U.S. inflation only	Exposure to U.S. inflation only
Stability of type of tax	Continual risk of unilateral change in oil production areas	Increased risk in oil refining areas and ocean transport	Little risk of basic change	Little risk of basic change
Stability of tax rate	Continual risk of unilateral change in oil production areas	Increased risk in oil refining areas and ocean transport	Little risk of basic change	Little risk of basic change
Stability of banking system	Exposure to more unstable foreign banking system	Exposure to more unstable foreign banking system	Exposure to U.S. system only	Exposure to U.S. system only
Stability of returns	Exposure to more unstable world environment	Exposure to more unstable world environment	Exposure to U.S. environment only	Exposure to U.S. environment only

Table 10A-4
Environmental Uncertainty in the Energy Industry

Environmental Uncertainties	Production Sector	Distribution Sector	Marketing Sector	Conversion Sector
Stability of geothermal drilling technology	Continual risk owing to state-of-the-art technology	Not applicable	Not applicable	Little risk of basic change
Stability of coal gasification technology	Continual risk owing to state-of-the-art technology	Limited risk of change in oil refining and ocean transportation	Not applicable	Little risk of basic change
Stability of shale oil extraction	Continual risk owing to state-of-the-art technology	Limited risk of change in oil refining and ocean transportation	Little risk of basic change	Little risk of basic change
Stability of current production methods	Continual risk owing to breakthroughs required in secondary recovery methods	Limited risk of change in oil refining and ocean transportation	Little risk of basic change	Little risk of basic change
Stability of OPEC nations	Continual risk because of control of large market sector	Limited risk of change in oil refining and ocean transportation	Little risk of basic change	Limited risk of basic change
Stability of accepting substantial quantities of foreign oil	Continual risk owing to no supertanker ports	Limited risk of change in oil refining and ocean transportation	Little risk of basic change	Little risk of basic change

Table 10A-5
Social Uncertainty in the Energy Industry

Social Uncertainties	Production Sector	Distribution Sector	Marketing Sector	Conversion Sector
Population	Foreign and U.S.	Foreign and U.S.	U.S. only	U.S. only
Stability of population	Continual risk of change in oil production areas	Continual risk of change in oil production areas	Much slower risk of change	Much slower risk of change
Change in economic status	Continual exposure to higher rate of change	Continual exposure to higher rate of change	Little risk of basic change	Little risk of basic change
Stability of birthrate	Continual risk of change in birthrate	Continual risk of change in birthrate	Birthrate leveling off	Birthrate leveling off

11

Southern California Edison Company

In this chapter the strategic planning process of Sourthern California Edison (SCE) Company will be discussed in detail. SCE is a major public utility located in Rosemead, California, a Los Angeles suburb. It serves 7.5 million people in a 50,000-square-mile area north of San Diego. It does not serve Los Angeles, for service in that city is provided by a municipally owned utility. In the 1977 *Fortune* listing of the fifty largest utilities, it ranked eighth with $4.95 billion in assets, $1.82 billion in operating revenue, and $222 million in net income. SCE owns and operates 36 hydroelectric plants, 12 fossil-fueled steam electric generating plants, two combustion turbine plants, and one diesel electric generating plant in central and sourthern California. SCE owns a majority interest in and operates the San Onofre Nuclear Generating Station in California and the Mohave Generating Station in Nevada.

Corporate Planning Process

Historically SCE has been a highly centralized organization. This section will describe in detail how the corporate planning process (see Figure 11-1, page 98) is carried out in the company.

The purpose of planning at Southern California Edison is explained as follows in the corporate planning manual:

The purpose of planning is to increase management effectiveness by providing managers with a tool for anticipating and responding to future changes in the business environment. For the corporation, planning is designed to provide a sense of direction for managers.

The four most commonly cited reasons for planning are: (1) to offset uncertainty and change, (2) to focus attention on objectives, (3) to gain an economical operation, and (4) to facilitate the exercise of control.

Formal corporate planning is a method of determining the optimum allocation of resources to attain desired objectives which involves the use of written planning policies, procedures, and guidelines. It includes planning schedules, the preparation of written plans, an approval process, and periodic reviews for monitoring implementation and taking corrective action. Often, formal corporate planning includes the use of a planning staff to develop the process.

Edison's planning system is designed to be sequential in its operating form, which is desirable. Conceptually, there is a logical series of activities which must be

97

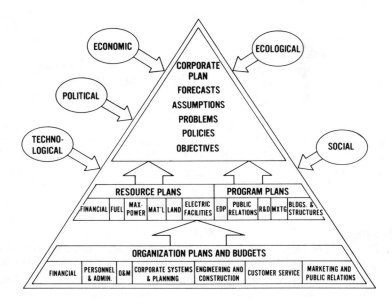

Figure 11-1. Corporate Planning Framework at Southern California Edison Company.

accomplished to provide integrated planning. All the elements and components of Edison's planning system are transmitted to officers and managers except for the organization plans. The purpose is to provide inter-organizational consistency in planning. Because organization plans are primarily used by managers and officers within an organizational unit, only information on projects requiring inter-organizational coordination is shared. As a result, once a manager understands the concepts of planning, the free flow of planning data should facilitate improved effectiveness.

An important consideration of any planning system is that it be responsive to new areas of management concern. The system itself must be adaptable and responsive to changing management requirements. If the planning system is to continue to provide integrated response to change, it must be dynamic enough to accommodate and incorporate these changes.

As Edison's planning system has matured, top management involvement has increased with the Management Committee taking a more active role in managing the planning system. Presently, the committee reviews all plans and is actively involved in the formulation and approval process of each element in the process. The committee has evolved from an interested observer to an active participant in the formal planning process.

In the past, the interdependence and continuity of the elements in the formal corporate planning process at Edison have not been important considerations. These factors were implicit in the planning system. As the focus of the various elements are brought together, the relevance of integration in the planning system grows in importance.[1]

Management Committee

The Management Committee was established in 1973. Its predecessor, the Corporate Planning Committee, was originally established in 1965 and reported to the vice presidents in charge of enginering, finance, and rates, through the manager of system development. The purpose of this committee at that time was to be advisory to the manager of system development for:

I. The annual development of the Ten-Year Master Plan for System Expansion incorporating physical, operational, and financial programs, and including:
    1. The evaluation of long-range system expansion plans in terms of corporate economics giving consideration to future financing requirements, rates of return, and earnings for Common stock.
    2. The forecasting of future revenues and the analysis of revenue trends as compared to revenue requirements in order to assess the probable future adequacy of the form and level of existing and/or proposed rate structures.
    3. The evaluation of selected changes in the character of system development and in corporate policy in terms of overall costs and economic impact: Such as the increased use of underground facilities, proposed changes in marketing programs and policies, strategic alternatives of power supply, etc.
II. The periodic development of short-range financial plans including assessments of alternative physical, operational and financial programs.

To assure adequate communication and coordination between all departments and divisions accountable for long- and short-range planning of physical facilities, financial and rate programs so that such plans may be measured in terms of total corporate needs and goals.[2]

The membership of the committee was later changed and consisted of the president of the company, who acted as committee chairman, two senior vice presidents; and four vice presidents. The manager of corporate planning acted as secretary of the committee, and the corporate planning staff provided support.

In mid-1973, a major reorganization of corporate committees in the company resulted in the transformation of the Corporate Planning Committee into the Management Committee. The nature and functions of the Management Committee are summarized below:

1. Provide direction to the company corporate planning, budgeting, and operations including the following:
    a. Direct policy formulation and review selected corporate issues which require resolution.
    b. Review corporate assumptions and other estimates of future business conditions.

   c. Review and evaluate corporate planning/budgeting policies and guidelines and direct changes to planning/budgeting process.

   d. Review and approve organization plans and function and manpower budgets.

   e. Review proposals for and minitor implementation of companywide programs and plans.

2. Review and approve executive development and replacement plans and programs.

3. Review and approve salary budgets, executive-level performance appraisals, and executive merit increases (except for corporate officers).

4. Review corporate problem issues and approve actions to solve corporate problems.

The manager of corporate planning acted as secretary of the Management Committee. The secretary, with the chairman's guidance, is responsible for arranging staff work necessary to support the committee, reporting the status of actions initiated by the committee, preparing Management Committee meetings, notifying appropriate personnel of these meetings, and recording and distributing minutes of meetings.

Corporate Planning Staff

In 1968, the Corporate Planning Staff was established to direct the corporate planning process of SCE. Additionally, they were to provide support to the Corporate Planning Committee, which is now termed the Management Committee and which now consists of the chairman of the board, the president, and two executive vice presidents.

The staff is responsible for the functional coordination of the corporate planning process, which includes: (1) responsibility for directing the formulation and publication of corporate assumptions and policies, (2) responsibility for the coordination and administration of SCE program plans, (3) responsibility for developing and implementing organizational planning in SCE, and (4) responsibility for administering the corporate problem-solving process.

The major role of the staff is to coordinate and integrate the corporate planning process in SCE. They initiate planning, foster innovation, counsel other parts of the organization in their planning, and provide studies as required to improve the corporate planning process and to aid management in the decision-making process.

Perhaps the most important function of the Corporate Planning Staff is to provide staff services for the weekly scheduled meetings of the Management Committee. Under the direction of the chairman, the manager of corporate planning is responsible for analyzing and recommending changes in the planning and budgeting procedures and such other work as is required to support the activities of the Management Committee.

Corporate Overall Plan

When corporate planning was initially established at Southern California Edison, a corporate plan for the entire company was developed and published. It was soon decided that an effective corporate planning effort at SCE did not require an overall corporate plan since this was too general for effective assistance to management. So it was dropped from the corporate planning process.

Corporate Objectives

Southern California Edison has no formally stated corporate objectives. Top management sees no clear purpose in making a long list of corporate goals that would have little meaning. They prefer to have more specific goals stated in the major organizational units. Objectives are developed within the program, resource, and organization plans so that SCE has multiple objectives which are very specific, and often quantitative. What the company does not have is one major list of general goals called the corporate objectives.

Corporate Assumptions

Corporate assumptions have been part of the formal planning system at SCE since formal planning was initiated. Originally the assumptions were updated annually. As the planning process evolved, it became apparent that the assumptions should be updated more frequently, and a semiannual review was instituted by the Corporate Planning Staff.

Assumptions are defined in the corporate planning manual of SCE as

estimates of some future event or condition which have a significant impact on the preparation and implementation of the corporation's plans or the conduct of its operations. It is a probable development that cannot be determined with accuracy and over which there is little or no significant control.[3]

The purpose of corporate assumptions is to provide a mutual framework for developing plans by reducing the risk and cost in decision making by attempting to minimize surprise. Corporate assumptions are the basis for developing corporate objectives, program plans, and organizational plans. Individual managers and planning coordinators are responsible for utilizing the corporate assumptions when developing their plans and projects and for analyzing their impact. By utilizing corporate assumptions in the formal planning program, interorganizational planning consistency is improved.

Several changes were enacted in 1972 when the role of corporate assumptions in the SCE planning process was analyzed. One major change was to involve not only professional staff personnel but also officers and operating managers in developing the corporate assumptions during the semiannual review.

SCE has a very detailed set of corporate assumptions. The following subjects are covered: (1) social attitudes and values, (2) political trends, (3) human resources, (4) economic business conditions, (5) electric system growth, (6) technological change, and (7) fuel resources. See Appendix 11A.

Corporate Policy

Prior to 1971, corporate policy in Southern California Edison existed in many forms. At that time, the Corporate Planning Staff initiated the coordination of corporate policy. Prior to the Corporate Planning Staff initiation, SCE policy could be found in bulletins, operating letters, memoranda, directives, and many other undocumented and uncoordinated forms.

The following will describe certain aspects of SCE policy:

1. Levels
2. Format
3. Purpose
4. Development
5. Review
6. Distribution
7. Implementation
8. Summary

Levels

There are two basic levels of policy at SCE: corporate policy and departmental policy. Corporate policy is a statement of the company's chief executive officer or president, stated as a principle and supported by action rules. Corporate policy is stated in broad terms. It serves as a guideline to daily decision making, and it must remain flexible to compensate for rapidly changing conditions.

Departmental policy is analagous to corporate policy, but is stated by the responsible manager or officer rather than the chief executive officer or the president. Corporate policy is stated in detailed terms to support that corporate policy which provides interdepartmental guidelines. Although departmental policy must comply with corporate policy, intradepartmental policy may exist without guidelines provided by higher-level corporate policy.

Format

Each policy statement will consist of two parts. The first will be a statement of principle; it is followed by the second part, rules of action. The statement of principle should express the judgment supporting management's intended actions. Action rules should be application-oriented to serve as a useful guide for managers and employees.

Purpose

The purposes of a corporate policy are to (1) assist exercising executive leadership, (2) provide guidelines to achieve consistent decision making, (3) provide greater delegation of decision making lower within the organization, and (4) communicate principles to guide management decisions and employee action.

Development

Corporate policies are developed by the officers responsible for the functional area concerned with the policy. The chief executive officer or the president approves all corporate policies. The vice president of finance assisted by the Corporate Planning Staff coordinates the development and publication of a body of corporate policy in conjunction with the organization having functional authority over each policy area.

The development of a corporate policy begins with the determination of need. The need might be to provide new decision-making guidelines to management on some specific activity or to revise existing guidelines in some area to eliminate a restriction that may be impeding specific results. The need for policy may develop in a wide variety of situations such as the economic environment, changes in company operations, or organizational plans.

The preliminary policy draft is then coordinated by the Corporate Planning Staff. This coordination includes substantial effort within SCE and checking with other companies, both utility and nonutility. The draft must also be checked to ensure compliance with all regulatory agencies to which SCE is subject, such as the California Public Utilities Commission, Federal Power Commission, and the Securities and Exchange Commission.

Policy formulation at SCE has been found to be much more effective when many supervisors and managers are involved. Their involvement in the policy formulation process should increase their understanding of the policies after they are implemented and should lead them to voluntarily communicate their intent and monitor their achieved results. After the proposed policy draft is considered satisfactory to the appropriate department managers, it is then reviewed by senior management.

Review

The formal review of the policy statement is initiated when it is examined by the officers of the organization to which it is applicable. After the initial work on the policy by middle management, further review continues on the policy developed at lower management levels. The appropriate reviewing officers contribute to the policy development based on their experience and expertise. This effort is considered to be very important since the corporate policies and later revisions will probably remain in force during the life of the company.

The results of the reviews by various responsible officers are then examined by the manager and officer responsible for development of the policy. The results of this examination and the disposition of the comments are sent back to the reviewing officers.

Disagreements that arise during the process are resolved at a meeting between the officer responsible for the policy statement, the officers challenging it, and the vice president of finance. If the disagreement cannot be resolved, it is then forwarded to the president of the SCE.

After the policy formulations and review phases are completed, the policies are finally reviewed and approved by the president, chief executive, and chairman of the board. Then they are published in the SCE manuals.

Distribution

Published corporate policy statements are distributed directly to officers and department managers in accordance with a mandatory distribution list maintained by the Corporate Planning Staff. Each member of management is responsible for being familiar with them and discussing the key areas of concern at staff meetings.

Each organization or department has an Edison System of Manuals coordinator who provides for the policy needs of those employees not covered on the mandatory distribution list. He or she provides policy statements and procedures for department employees on a need-to-know basis.

Implementation

After broad action rules are published which tell what SCE is doing regarding a subject policy and why it is being done, specific guidelines on implementation are set. This information is contained in corporate procedures. Corporate procedures set forth areas of responsibility and authority and provide detailed information for the user. Each corporate procedure lists a series of related steps or tasks expressed in chronological order to achieve a specific purpose or to follow a specific policy. Corporate procedures are methods, techniques, and detailed ways by and through which policies are followed.

When more detailed direction is required by personnel in an individual department, the responsible manager is delegated authority from the executive office to provide the required direction in a departmental policy. If more than one organization or department is affected, a corporate policy is required.

Summary

The policy formulation process of Southern California Edison Company is a lengthy one. However, policies can be approved in a priority order, which enables management to direct initial efforts toward the major problem areas while systematically accomplishing them all. SCE planning personnel find the major problem in policy formulation is overcoming the initial reluctance to get started. Policy development becomes easier once this initial reluctance passes and polices are determined and implemented to assist in making operating decisions in a particular problem area.

Program and Resource Plans

Program and Resource Plans are established to focus attention on major activities of Southern California Edison which are of a critical nature and require ongoing top management direction. The following paragraphs will describe certain aspects of SCE Program and Resource Plans.

History

A Program and Resource Plan was initially defined as a planning document which concentrated on a work project, business strategy, or resource requirement of major importance to SCE. Program and Resource Plans usually require the cooperative effort of several departments.

The purpose of the plans was to focus management attention on programs critical to the growth and success of SCE. Each plan was established as follows:

1. Summary
2. Evaluation of current situation
3. Forecasts and assumptions
4. Plan objectives
5. Projects and recommendations

The Management Committee initiated program and resource planning at SCE. They sent a letter to the officer responsible for each plan requesting its preparation. The letter included a set of guidelines to use in preparation of the plan, an evaluation of the previous year's plan, and a plan coordinator to assist.

There are currently eleven Program and Resource Plans. The original set of plans in 1968 included Electrical Facilities, Fuel Supply, Manpower, Manager Development, Financial, Marketing, Material Management, Forecasting and Environmental Analysis, Comprehensive Edison Information system, and Buildings and Structures. Seven of the original ten programs continued into 1973. The remaining three were changed as follows. Forecasting and Environmental Analysis was discontinued as a plan in 1969 and was included in Electrical Systems Planning. The Comprehensive Edison Information System Plan was discontinued in 1969 and placed on the corporate problem list. It was renamed Accounting and Management Reporting and resolved in 1972. The Buildings and Structure Plan was discontinued and placed on the corporate problem list in 1969, renamed Building Space Planning and Management, and resolved in 1971.

Three new plans were added during 1972: Research and Development, Public Relations, and Electrical Data Processing. The Envionrmental Program Plan was added in 1973.

Guidelines

The following guidelines limit Program and Resource Plans to projects that are critically important to SCE:

a. The absence of ongoing direction by top management will result in major problem issues which will have an adverse effect on the company's financial position, will restrict operating capabilities and/or will reduce the company's ability to respond to changes in their external environment.

b. The functional activities represents a major portion of corporate resources.

c. Coordination and communication of such activities will produce a greater sense of corporate priorities and improved utilization of corporate resources.

d. Existing management procedures, such as organization plans, task forces and committees for coordinating activities, do not exist or would be inadequate.[4]

Controls

Program plans require the following cost and management controls.

(1) The organization submitting the proposal will estimate costs and benefits. Prior to placing the item on the Management Committee agenda, the Corporate Planning Staff, with budget director input, will coordinate a review of the recommendation and cost estimates.

(2) The Management Committee should establish two resource limitations: one for resources expended developing the plan and one for implementing the plan.

(3) Periodic progress reports will be made to the Management Committee. The Management Committee has the responsibility for monitoring the plan, for implementation, for evaluating status reports, and for coordinating required reviews by the Management Committee.

(4) Organization plans should include objectives to reflect the responsibility of each organization developing or implementing a program plan. They should also include function and manpower budget references.

Process

The Program Planning Process provides the means to study and evaluate alternatives resulting in objectives in key areas affecting the company's future. It operates on an annual cycle with completion dates for program plan revisions set throughout the year. A brief description of the process follows.

(1) *Identification of key result areas.* Initially, a key result area (major work project, business strategy, or resource requirement) must be identified. Any officer or manager can recommend an issue to the Management Committee. After the area is identified, it is assigned to an officer with the most logical functional responsibilities with the approval of the Management Committee. Then the responsible officer designates a program plan coordinator to coordinate the development of the plan.

(2) *Drafting the scope of the plan.* Next, the key result areas must be refined to further establish the scope, to prepare a timetable for first-draft

completion, to define the relation of the plan to other plans, and to identify component parts of the plan. The scope is then approved by the Management Committee.

(3) *Preparation of the plan.* Next the plan is formalized by going through the planning process. The current situation is analyzed, forecasts and assumptions are developed, and projects and recommendations are enumerated. Detailed management responsibilities and estimated manpower resources are included in the objectives. Projects and recommendations list required facilities costs, benefits, and required changes in organization and policy.

(4) *Approval by committees.* Now the plan is forwarded to the Management Committee for review, concept approval, and approval of order-of-magnitude cost estimates, but not authorization for specific project expenditures. Individual projects and recommendations are approved by appropriate budget committees. The Operational Expenditure Review Committee authorizes operational expenditure through organizational plans and the Plant Expenditures Review Committee authorizes plant expenditures through the various projects identified in each program plan.

(5) *Implementation.* The responsible officer receives the authority to implement the plan when the Management Committee approves it. Organizational lines can be crossed to establish work relationships required to complete the plan.

(6) *Progress reports and annual reviews.* The responsible officer reports on progress made developing the plan. The plan is reviewed annually by the Management Committee to determine its continuing responsiveness.

(7) *Relationship to organization plans.* Program plans provide corporate direction by establishing key objectives for organizational planning purposes. They also provide a method of establishing organization planning priorities and cooperative planning efforts by several departments.

Organizational Jurisdiction

Jurisdiction at Southern California Edison is the "scope of responsibility assigned to an organizational unit." It defines the areas of accountability and describes the functions to be performed by an organizational unit. A separate jurisdiction statement or committee guide is prepared for each major organizational unit and corporate committee and is approved by the chief executive officer or the president. Each officer has the responsibility to initiate and prepare statements and guides for organizational units and committees under his/her direction.

The process of establishing and formalizing responsibilities of individual organizational units provides management with a tool to obtain a clear understanding of the purpose, scope, and functions of these organizations. Publication of jurisdiction statements and committee guides provides a vehicle for communicating organizational responsibilities and relationships at SCE.

The vice president of finance, with the assistance of the Corporate Planning Staff, was responsible for coordinating the development, review, approval, and publication of jurisdiction statements and committee guides. The Corporate Planning Staff will establish standards, guidelines, and provide assistance to organizational units.

The following subsections will describe certain aspects of SCE organizational jurisdiction statements.

Process

The process of developing and updating jurisdiction statements and committee guides is a continuous one to ensure that publications reflect current responsibilities. Appropriate jurisdiction statements and committee guides must be updated and approved by the chief executive officer or president before the scope, purpose, or functions of an organization can be changed. Resource allocations resulting from these changes will be made after the change is approved.

The following process is used at SCE to update jurisdiction statements:

1. The responsible officer submits proposed changes to jurisdiction statements and committee guides to the vice president of finance.
2. The vice president of finance, with the assistance of the Corporate Planning Staff, reviews the proposal to determine if overlap or confusion with responsibilities and functions of existing organizations would result. Adherence to format and guidelines is also reviewed.
3. The vice president of finance works with the various organizations involved to resolve any differences which may occur. If differences exist which cannot be resolved, they are defined and referred to the chief executive officer or president for resolution.

In addition, any officer or manager in SCE may initiate a change in a jurisdiction statement by informing the vice president of finance. Then the problem will be resolved in accordance with the prescribed SCE procedures.

Individual organizations review their jurisdiction statements annually as part of the organization planning process. The Corporate Planning Staff also reviews them annually with the vice president of finance, the chief executive officer, and the president.

SCE provides its personnel with an effective description of jurisdiction statements and committee guides in the corporate planning manual:

Jurisdiction statements and committee guides provide a clear understanding of the responsibility, purpose, and major functions of organizations. They are concise, informative, factual and free from extraneous and redundant material. Precise, understandable terminology that describes what an organization does, not how it does it, should be used. Jurisdiction statements are not intended to be job descriptions and are not prepared for individual officers or managers. Statements and guides should include short, simple words and sentences and be written in the active tense using common terminology.[5]

Terminology

SCE has a precise set of definitions to use in jurisdiction statements. The following definitions from the corporate planning manual have been developed specifically at SCE for jurisdiction statements:

a. *Accountability*—Continuing obligation to perform work. Sufficient authority to perform work should accompany accountability. (Synonym: Responsibility)

b. *Advise*—See *recommend*.

c. *Analyze*—Examine a complex whole to separate and identify its constituent parts and their relationship. Implies responsibility for discovery of fact. (Synonym: Study)

d. *Approve*—Endorse or accept. Approval implies that the item being approved has the endorsement of the approving agency or person. Approval may still require authorization by somebody else. Note distinction between approve and authorize.

e. *Assist*—Help by providing service. Assistance involves providing aid, upon request, without exercise of authority.

f. *Authority*—Powers and rights to direct, to cause others to do work or to cause something to happen.

g. *Authorize*—To have final authority and accountability to take action. No other confirmation is required beyond authorization.

h. *Consult*—To give professional or technical advice or recommendations without exercise of authority.

i. *Control*—Continuously analyze differences between expected results and actual results, in order to evaluate actions and take corrective measures as necessary. Control implies the authority to direct.

j. *Coordinate*—Schedule, unify, integrate, and influence work without the authority to direct the work.

k. *Decide*—See *determine*.

l. *Determine*—Fix conclusively or authoritatively, settle or decide by choice among alternatives or possibilities. (Synonym: Decide)

m. *Develop*—Build by successive, orderly additions and make ready for use. Includes preparation. (Synonym: Establish)

n. *Direct*—Exercise authority that will require other persons to do work. To direct implies having authority to control and the power to take corrective action in case of divergence.[6]

Approval and Implementation

After the Corporate Planning Staff reviews proposed changes, they are presented to the Management Committee for approval. The officer who is responsible initiates appropriate revisions after approval.

SCE considers it to be both impractical and undesirable to centralize all organizational structure decisions. However, SCE feels there must be a checks-and-balance system which gives corporate management the control to ensure that changes in organizational structure are consistent with company strategy.

Reorganization

The following steps summarize the reorganization process at Southern California Edison.

(1) First, a meeting is set up by the responsible officer or manager. The meeting will include the following: managers or supervisors affected by the reorganization, the department coordinator for the change, a corporate planning representative, an employee relations representative, an ESM representative, and a comptroller's representative. The meeting will discuss the nature, scope, and objectives of the reorganization; time parameters; and assignment of general responsibilities for reorganization activity.

(2) Next, specific responsibilities should be documented by the department coordinator for the reorganization and assigned to all organization representatives needed to implement and expedite the change.

(3) The actual reorganization process commences after the assignment of specific responsibilities. The organization coordinator for the affected department prepares a time schedule to effectively coordinate the activities. This schedule provides each responsible person involved in the reorganization with a sequence of events.

Organizational Plans

Organizational Plans at Southern California Edison refer to short-range planning at the organizational level or unit. An organizational level or unit in SCE is any major functional department which would include finance, personnel, or customer service. Each organization in Southern California Edison prepares a plan with a one- to three-year time frame that does the following:

1. Identifies the portion of Southern California Edison's operation for which the organizational level or unit is responsible to plan and achieve results
2. Estimates significant future environmental changes, from corporate assumptions
3. Recommends new or revised corporate policies
4. Recommends new or revised Program and Resource Plans
5. Determines objectives to be achieved by the organizational level or unit to respond to environmental changes
6. Determines resources required by the organizational level or unit to achieve objectives

The following subsections describe certain aspects of SCE organization plans.

History

While the formal planning system was being developed at SCE, emphasis was placed on organizational plans by the Management Committee for several reasons. First, there was little formal planning expertise in the various organizations. Second, approximately forty plans had to be prepared. Third, since the program plans had evolved from a previous planning effort, they were ongoing planning activities.

As a result of the initial emphasis, the SCE planning process was too structured. In 1971 a less structured approach was taken. The Management Committee redistributed planning manpower and changed planning priorities to take a more balanced approach to formal training.

Two other significant changes were also made to improve the organizational planning process. First, the budgeting process was incorporated into the organizational planning process in 1970. Second, the president and chief executive officer conducted reviews of all organizational plans with managers and responsible officers.

Purpose

The major purpose of an organizational plan in SCE is to assist the managers in directing their organizations. The plans are their plan, developed to meet their needs, and serve to communicate the courses of action to be taken by their organization in performing its major function and achieving its objectives. The plan also provides senior management with decision-making information and other organizations with information required to respond effectively to the needs of the organization. It also highlights end results to accomplish rather than routine tasks to perform.

Scope

An organizational plan is a management tool which serves to communicate what courses of action an organization will take in performing major functions and achieving its goals. The scope of an organization plan includes the following:

1. The plan must communicate to the managers and supervisors within the organization the courses of action they are to take in contributing to the performance of the organization's major functions and the achievement of its objectives.
2. The plan must communicate to senior management, providing them with knowledge of the organization's courses of actions, so that they may make evaluations, judgments, and decisions.
3. The plan must communicate to other organizations involved so that they may react to provide the services and resources needed.

Process

There are four major steps, called the organizational planning process, involved in developing an organizational plan at SCE:

1. Evaluate the current situation.
2. Estimate future conditions and evaluate the impact.
3. Determine desired results and resources required.
4. Monitor the environment and evaluate progress.

Step One. The first step in the process involves an analysis of current business conditions and current problems of the organization, within the framework of the corporate assumptions. It also includes evaluation of current jurisdiction statements, corporate policies, organizational objectives, and resource expenditures.

A jurisdiction statement that defines areas of accountability and describes major functions to be performed has been developed for each major organizational level or unit. *Major functions* are defined as the portion of the total operation for which the organizational level or unit is to plan and achieve results. Any overlaps, omissions, or areas of confusion are identified by the organizational level or unit in the annual review of the jurisdiction statements.

Existing corporate policies are reviewed annually to ensure that they are not vague or conflicting and that they do not hinder the organizational level or unit in performing major functions or achieving stated objectives.

Organizational performance on previous objectives is evaluated annually to determine the effectiveness of the organizational level or unit and also to assist in identifying organizational strengths and weaknesses.

Step Two. The second step in the process involves estimating changes in the business environment and evaluating the organizational impact within the framework of the corporate assumptions.

The business environment of SCE includes the total of the conditions in which it operates: economic, social, political, ecological, and technological. Changes in the environment may have major impacts on the company's operations. Unforeseen changes may have disastrous effects. Each organizational level or unit must consider the scope and direction of future business environment change, as stated in the corporate assumptions, and the potential effects upon the organization.

The evaluation of the impact of a change in the business environment, as stated in the corporate assumptions, on an organizational level or unit is determined by estimating the magnitude of the resulting problems that will face the organization.

Step Three. The third step in organizational planning involves determining how the organization will respond to the problems foreseen. Changes in organizational structure, operating procedures, and resource allocations may be required in response to these problems.

Changes in the business environment may have several impacts upon the organizational level or unit; activities may be increased or decreased; new priorities may be established; workloads may increase or decrease; major resource expenditures may not correspond to major functions; and jurisdiction statements may need redefining.

Changes in the business environment may require revised corporate policies. Existing corporate policies may be vague, conflicting, or restrictive to the organizational level or unit.

One of the most important and fundamental elements of the organizational plan is setting objectives. Emphasis is placed on achieving results rather than on performing activities.

Objectives have many applications in the process. Several examples follow.

1. Objectives oriented to work that the organizational level or unit performs in carrying out its major functions, including project-type work,

such as engineering projects, construction projects, and system development projects

2. Objectives pertaining to managerial responsibilities, such as planning, organizing, staffing, directing, controlling, coordinating, and innovating

3. Objectives established as a result of responsibility assigned to the organization via corporate problems, program plans, resource plans, executive directives, and assignments by a corporate committee or task force

Next the organizational level or unit must decide what resources it requires to perform its major function and achieve its objective. The resource requirements are documented in a budget. The budget approval by top management authorizes the allocation of the resources to an organization, and provides final approval for the organizational plan.

Step Four. The last step in the process involves implementing the developed plans. Since the environment is continually changing, each organization must continually monitor the corporate assumptions about the environment and modify its plans as necessary. SCE personnel believe an organizational level or unit could achieve every objective during the year yet finds its problems greatly increased by its failure to respond to change. Therefore, organizations must continuously evaluate progress toward their objectives. Deviation from plan must be found quickly, and corrective action must be taken. Most SCE organizations accomplish this on a quarterly basis.

Corporate Problems

Corporate problems at Southern California Edison are major problem issues of a critical nature which must be solved without delay. The corporate problem-solving process provides officers and managers with a tool for identifying major problems and also for requesting the resources necessary to resolve them.

Guidelines

Corporate problem issues are limited by the following guidelines:

1. Continued existence of the problem issue will have an adverse effect on the company's financial position, will restrict operating capabilities, and/or will reduce the company's ability to respond to changes in the external environment.

2. Existing management procedures such as policy formulation, program plans, the systems development cycle, organization plans, etc., do not provide adequate methods for solution.

History

The number of corporate problems has varied in the past to as many as thirty issues. There are three corporate problems in progress: demand control, warehousing and distribution, and multipurpose mapping.

The final resolution of corporate problem issues takes various forms. Some are solved while others have either been dropped as corporate problems or been reassigned to a specific organization to solve through its organization planning process. Initially, issues were not clearly defined, top management participation was lacking, and accountability for solving the problems, although clearly defined, was seldom emphasized.

Problem-Solving Steps

These steps are followed in corporate problem solving.

(1) *Problem identification.* The first step is identifying the problem. After identification, it is presented to the Management Committee for adoption as a corporate problem. After adoption, the Management Committee assigns the corporate problem to a company officer with functional responsibility for the problem area who then designates a problem coordinator.

(2) *Developing the solution.* The coordinator develops a study plan which describes how the problem will be solved and the resources required. The officer and coordinator are responsible for developing the problem solution when the study plan is approved. The problem solution is presented in a report called a "project memorandum," which includes alternatives considered, a recommendation, and a detailed implementation plan.

(3) *Implementation and close-out.* The problem solution is implemented after Management Committee approval. The responsible officer directs the implementation phase during execution of the implementation plan. The solution of a corporate problem may be handled several ways. Objectives may be established in the appropriate organization or program plans, a special project may be established, or it may require a new program plan.

A corporate problem is considered resolved when the project memorandum is approved by the Management Committee. Close-out may occur before, during, or after implementation of the solution, at the chairman's discretion. Close-out does not affect the responsible officer's obligation to report on the results of the implementation.

(4) *Evaluation.* After a reasonable time, the corporate planning staff will request a status report from the responsible officer. Results that are significantly different from those expected will be brought to the attention of the committee chairman.

Controls

Various cost and management controls are utilized for corporate problems.

The Corporate Planning Staff coordinates a review of the recommendations and cost estimates included in the proposal before it is placed on the Management Committee's agenda.

The Management Committee establishes resource limitations for both studies and implementing solutions.

The assigned responsible officer makes periodic reports to the Management Committee on the status of his or her resources.

The Corporate Planning Staff monitors the progress of corporate problem solutions, monitors status, and coordinates necessary reviews by the Management Committee.

Organizational plans of each organization involved in the study or implementation of a corporate problem include objectives, function budget, and manpower budget references.

Summary

The strategic planning process of a major United States electric public utility operating in a rapidly changing environment has been presented. The reader can examine in great detail how complex the process is and how it works. In the next chapter, the SCE strategic planning process will be analyzed using several different standards.

Notes

1. Southern California Edison Company, Corporate Planning Manual.
2. Ibid.
3. Ibid.
4. Ibid.
5. Ibid.
6. Ibid.

Appendix 11A:
Southern California
Edison Company
Corporate Assumptions

Corporate Assumptions are essential components in the development of program and organizational plans. They are estimates of future conditions over which the Company has little or no control and which may have a significant impact on the preparation and implementation of the Company's plans.

These assumptions have been formulated for use only as a starting point in the planning process. They should not be regarded as forecasts of events which are certain to occur, nor as events which the Company necessarily considers desirable. As more information becomes available, these assumptions will be modified or eliminated to reflect changing conditions.

Each assumption should be reviewed to determine what impact the expected development may have on the Company and a particular organizational unit. Once the extent of this impact is ascertained, consideration should be given to formulating objectives which will minimize the magnitude of the impact. Not all assumptions are relevant to each organizational unit.

All Corporate Assumptions will be reviewed and updated on a periodic basis. The Corporate Planning Staff is responsible for coordinating these reviews. Each officer is responsible for assessing the impact of all assumptions on his or her areas of responsibility.

Social Attitudes and Values

Attitudes and expectations regarding the purpose, function, and role of business are changing. Criticism and distrust of large business organizations will increase. The public will assign more responsibility to business for improving social conditions and the environment. The public will demand more and better communication from business and government concerning their accomplishments.

Regulatory bodies will become increasingly affected by public demands to halt the upward spiral of rates and to expand utility environmental and social objectives.

Near-term reductions in *pollution levels* and continued expenditures for aesthetic and other environmental purposes will be approved by regulatory action, regardless of whether or not the public wishes to pay for the increased costs.

Due to the nature of the public's view of *nuclear hazards*, conventional risk assessments, based upon numerical probabilities, will have limited effectiveness in allaying public concern.

Public criticism, questioning, and challenging of *advertising* will continue to increase.

Quality-of-life considerations will receive increasing attention.

Political Trends

SCE will experience increasing pressure to *limit energy consumption growth* to areas that are socially and environmentally acceptable.

SCE will be required by regulatory agencies to *increase the involvement* of citizens and conservation groups in electric facility planning, rate proceedings, and other hearings.

As pollution regulations become more stringent, SCE will experience increasing difficulty in obtaining required construction and operation permits. Those obtained will be contingent upon increasingly costly and rigid compliance plans and schedules.

There will be increasingly stringent discharge *requirements* concerning trace elements, chemical, sewage, and thermal discharge to fresh, coastal, and ground waters.

Future *development of unused land and recycling of presently developed land* will be subject to more controls.

Increasing pressure will be exerted to involve both the FPC and PUC in questions of *employment discrimination* as they relate to rate cases.

Public groups and government agencies will exert increasing pressure on SCE to make use of *interconnections, diversity, inverted rate structures, and off-peak rates* in an effort to reduce energy usage and maximize use of generating capacity.

Effects of the *energy crisis and environmental constraints* will result in increased political interest in energy forecasting techniques.

The importance of *regional governmental* units will increase relative to that of local governmental units. State and federal entities will exert greater influence over governmental functions at both local and regional levels.

Human Resources

Greater pressures will be exerted by governmental agencies and community groups to increase *employment and promotion opportunities* for minorities, females, veterans, and individuals in older age groups.

Unions will attempt to extend representation to *technical, clerical, and professional groups* not currently represented.

As the workforce becomes younger and increasing numbers of experienced personnel are hired, greater pressure will be exerted for *changes in the mix of benefits and wages.* These changes may include provisions for more options on the part of individual employees.

Employees expecting and demanding more *personal satisfaction* from their jobs and more *recognition from the Company and the Union* will utilize the grievance and arbitration procedures and state and federal agencies to a greater extent.

Due to the *increased enrollment in law schools,* there will be an influx of attorneys into the corporate management structure and an increase in the level of adverse-position activity.

Employees will continue to press for increased *personal rights of privacy, individuality, and nontraditional modes of behavior and expression.*

Employees will continue to press for more *responsible and less structured job assignments.*

Governmental agencies and labor unions will take actions to increase their involvement in safety programs and work practices.

The advantages of *replacing labor with equipment* will increase.

Economic/Business Conditions

Real personal income in California will increase at an annual rate of between 3 and 4 percent.

Costs of new issues of securities will be as follows:

Bonds	7-8 percent
Preferred Stocks	7-8 percent
Convertible Preferred and Preference Stock	6-7 percent
Price/Earnings Ratio (Times)	10-15 percent

The Social Security tax rates will be 6.05 percent for 1978-1980 and 6.15 percent for 1981-1982. The wage base for application of the above percentages is $10,800 for 1973, $12,000 for 1974 and subsequent years, automatically escalated for benefit increases when the cost of living rises 3 percent or more.

Investors will demand *increasing return on equity* as inflation continues to erode their purchasing power.

The *average land value* appreciation will be 6 percent, compounded annually.

Technological Change

Government regulation and public pressure for *improvements in safety* will increase as technology advances.

Improvements will be made in dc *transmission* components and various methods of underground transmission by 1980, which will result in cost reductions.

Helium turbines for high-temperature, gas-cooled reactor application will be available by 1980.

The technical feasibility of conversion of *solar energy* in land-based plants will be established by 1980, but commercial application will not occur before 2000.

The technical feasibility of *fusion* will be established by 1980, but commercial application will not occur before 2000.

Pressure will increase for both gas and electric utilities to develop and market *solar energy systems* for space and water heating.

Electric System Growth

Due to environmental pressures, greater use of *combined-cycle plants* will be made through 1979.

The *undergrounding* of 66-kV transmission lines in selective urban locations and 220-kV transmission lines in selective metropolitan locations will become increasingly necessary because of environmental and land use considerations.

Restrictions on coastal and populace area *facility siting*, plus *public attitudes* toward nuclear hazards and waste disposal, will increase the difficulty of obtaining economically feasible and environmentally compatible sites.

Increasing requirements for facility environmental impact reports will continue to lengthen *lead times*.

The inability of electric utilities to nationally meet load demand, plus a growing need for new sources of revenue, will increase the *interest of local governments* in owning and operating their own electric systems.

Municipal utilities will increasingly desire to participate with SCE in construction of new generating facilities.

SCE will be able to obtain permission to begin construction of *critical generation facilities*. However, there exists a high probability that during the next decade there will be periods of inadequate generation to meet the system load demand.

Aesthetic construction of subtransmission and transmission lines will be required for the majority of the lines in urban and suburban areas.

Pollution abatement equipment and facilities may significantly increase energy demand.

Fuel Resources

Gas

Environmental constraints will require the use of all available gas supplies and will increase the difficulty of providing adequate backup fuel.

Fuel Oil

Instability in major oil-supplying countries will necessitate provisions be made in Company planning for occasional *dislocation of supplies*.

A three-year lead time will be required to provide a sufficient quantity of *turbine fuel* of the required quality for use in gas-turbine and combined-cycle generating facilities.

The cost to provide a suitable *liquid fuel* for use in gas turbines will range from 10 to 15 percent over conventional fuel oil.

Low-sulphur fuel oil supplies will be available in sufficient quantities to supply requirements.

Coal

Coal priced up to 40 cents per million Btu, within a radius of 700 miles, will be economically competitive for generation and transmission of electric power to Southern California.

During the period from 1975 to 1982, *coal priced* up to 35 cents per million Btu, within a radius of 1200 miles, will be economically feasible for generation and transmission of electric power to Southern California.

Nuclear

Additions to free world *uranium production capability* will keep pace with demand for nuclear reactor fuels through 1980.

Prior to 1985, *plutonium* will be used primarily as a recycle fuel in light-water reactors and will range in cost from $7.00 to $7.50 per gram of fissile Pu. Rising uranium concentrate prices and fast breeder projects are expected to increase the value to above $10.00 during the 1980s.

12 An Analysis of the Southern California Edison System

In earlier chapters, there was a detailed introductory discussion of strategic planning. The energy environment from 1960 to 1975 was described with the uncertainties in the various sectors of the energy industry. Finally, Southern California Edison, a company in the energy industry, was described and its corporate planning process was discussed in detail.

In this chapter, a complete analysis will be made of the corporate planning system of this company. The analysis will be conducted using the following criteria:

1. Concept of strategic planning as originated in the Business Policy Department of the Harvard Business School
2. George Steiner's five key dimensions of business planning
3. Peter Drucker's definition of strategic planning
4. Peter Drucker's eight objectives for strategic plans

A final summary in matrix form follows each criteria section and provides an overview of the strategic planning process according to that criterion.

The strategic planning process of a firm is usually a highly individualized undertaking. It depends upon such variables as the business the firm is in, the time period a formal planning process has been utilized, and the involvement and support of top management, to only mention a few. Therefore, it would not be too surprising to ascertain major differences in the formal planning system of companies. These differences may exist not only in the structure of the system but also in its objectives or goals.

Business Policy Concept

The first academic construct which will be utilized to analyze the strategic planning system will be the concept of strategic planning developed in the Business Policy Department of the Harvard Business School. This concept originated in the 1950s and has been under development since then. Further work on the business policy concept has been done at the Graduate School of Business Administration of The University of Michigan.

The business policy concept of strategic planning includes eight components:

1. Identification of the opportunities and risks in the environment, including the essential economic and technical characteristics of the industry, trends suggesting changes in those characteristics, and the nature of industrial competition
2. Identification of the resources of the organization, including the principal strengths and weaknesses as evidenced by the ability to compete within the industry
3. Identification of the personal values and aspirations of management and employees of the organization who must contribute to the strategy to make it effective
4. Identification of the legitimate interests of other segments of society which must be recognized within the strategy
5. Reconciliation of the characteristics, trends, and nature of competition within the environment; the strengths and weaknesses within the resources; the personal values and aspirations of the management; and the acknowledged obligations to society into a final choice of purpose
6. Identification of the tasks necessary for the accomplishment of purpose and the assignment of technically qualified individuals and groups to these specialized tasks
7. Provision of an organizational structure, for authority definition and information distribution, to assist in the coordination and accomplishment of the specialized tasks
8. Provision of a set of organizational systems, for performance measurement, operational control, and individual motivation, to assist in the coordination and accomplishment of the specialized tasks.

Environmental Risks and Opportunities

In the strategic planning process of the Southern California Edison Company, the identification of environmental risks and opportunities is a distinct, explicit portion of the process. Extensive analysis is done on the economic and technical characteristics of the industry. Appendix 11A(1) identifies the economic/business conditions extant in the corporate assumptions of SCE, (2) includes corporate assumptions on technological change, and (3) provides corporate assumptions on fuel resources. SCE has a very broad, detailed list of corporate assumptions on which to base its strategic planning. The specific analysis of risks and opportunities is inherent in the organizational planning process and in program and resource plans.

Resources

The identification of resources, including principal strengths and weaknesses, is an integral part of the strategic planning system of SCE.

As program and organization plans are developed, an analysis is performed to determine the competitive strengths and weaknesses inherent at SCE. This analysis is a specific integral part of program and organizational planning. Before a plan can be approved, the specific basis of the unit's organization strengths and weaknesses must be delineated.

Personal Values

At SCE, the strategic planning system requires that the personal values and aspirations of the employees of the organization be taken into account. It is not an explicit part of the strategic planning process, but the overall corporate planning which is accomplished must take into account the personal values and aspirations of management. The regard with which management obviously holds its employees, as evidenced by its policies, infers that this is an effective process.

Society's Interests

The strategic planning process at SCE recognizes throughout the system the legitimate interests of other segments of society. This may be due to the "fish bowl" atmosphere in which a major public utility in Southern California must operate. However, societal interests are recognized and dealt with throughout the strategic planning process. Explicit acknowledgment is made in the corporate assumptions in Appendix 11A where societal attitudes and values, political trends, and human resources are discussed. In addition to these explicit listings in the corporate assumptions, which serve as a foundation for the strategic planning system, the corporate assumptions are recognized in the development of corporate policy and organization plans.

Reconciliation

The reconciliation of the characteristics, trends, and nature of competition within the environment, the strengths and weaknesses within the resources, the personal values and aspirations of management, and the acknowledged obligations to society come together in an explicit definition of purpose at SCE. The SCE corporate planning system succinctly establishes the organization plans, resources plans, and program plans, all based on realistic corporate assumptions. These corporate assumptions provide a basic foundation for all planning accomplished at SCE. Consequently, when the reconciliation process is accomplished, SCE has an effective relationship with all diverse variables in the strategic planning process precisely because they explicitly delineate and analyze the different variables.

Tasks

The identification of tasks necessary to accomplish the purpose of the corporation and the assignment of technically qualified individuals and groups to these specialized tasks is a substantial, explicit part of the SCE strategic planning system. As the organizational, resource, and program plans are developed, they explicitly set forth the tasks that must be accomplished and identify the resources. Responsibility is established in each of these plans, and the resources necessary to accomplish the task are identified. The entire thrust of the strategic planning system at SCE is to devote sufficient resources to those problems which are identified as substantive in the environment of SCE. Consequently, the identification of necessary tasks is implicitly and explicitly treated most adequately in the planning process.

Organizational Structure

A very specific, detailed organizational structure for authority definition and information distribution to assist in the coordination and accomplishment of specialized tasks is utilized at SCE. The basic ongoing organization, with the substantiation of program and organizational plans, provides a well-thought-out, established organizational structure. The organizational plans of SCE are utilized to determine requirements for a new organization as a corporate problem evolves through the corporate planning process, such as one involving R&D. The process allows a new organizational structure as one of the resolutions of the corporate problem in the formal planning process.

Organizational Systems

SCE has an effective set of organizational systems for performance-measurement operational control. This control evolves through the management committee. The management committee provides direction to the company corporate planning, budgeting, and operation, including direct policy formulation and review, review of corporate assumptions, review of budgeting policies, review and approval of organizational plans and function of manpower budgets and proposals for companywide programs and plans. By this very effective and detailed overall review of the corporate strategic planning process and the interwoven operating detail of SCE, the organizational system provides an impetus for the ongoing work of the corporation.

Summary

A summary of the business policy's eight components of strategic planning is found in Table 12-1.

Table 12-1
Summary Analysis of SCE Using Business Policy Criteria

Business Policy's Eight Components of Strategic Planning	SCE
1. Identify environmental risks and opportunities.	A separate, explicit part of the strategic planning process; part of organizational planning.
2. Identify organizational resources.	Integral part of program and organizational planning.
3. Identify personal values and aspirations of management and employees.	Although not an explicit part of the planning process, the corporate strategy evolves from top management considerations and values.
4. Identify legitimate interests of other segments of society which must be recognized.	Recognized throughout the strategic planning system including corporate assumptions on social attitudes and values; development of corporate policy and organizational plans.
5. Reconciliation of environment, resources, personal values of management, and acknowledged obligation of society into a formal choice of purpose.	Reconciliation of organization, resource, and program plans.
6. Identify necessary tasks.	Integral part of program and organizational plans.
7. Provide an organizational structure.	Objectives or program plans or organizational plans.
8. Provide organizational systems for performance measurement, operational controls, and industry motivation.	Planning system includes detailed controls on all aspects of the operational system.

George Steiner's Concept

In his major work on planning entitled *Top Management Planning*, George Steiner sets forth a useful method of classifying business plans. He refers to the five key dimensions of business planning: (1) organization, (2) elements, (3) time, (4) subject, and (5) characteristics. The organizational dimension of planning refers to the type of organizational planning involved (such as the corporation, subsidiary, division, department, or a project) and the type of organization that accomplishes planning within the company. The elements refer to the different components of planning, such as a rule, procedure, policy, or objective. Time refers to the time horizon of plans, such as short-, medium-, or long-range. Subject refers to the material covered in the plans, such as marketing, financial, or production. Characteristics refers to the properties of planning, such as flexible, rational, and written.

Organization

Formal planning at Southern California Edison is functionally directed by the Corporate Planning Staff. Essentially, the Corporate Planning Staff acts as a coordinator and an integrator for the corporate planning process. The group also initiates planning, stimulates innovation, and acts as a consultant for various functional groups in SCE that are developing plans.

The Corporate Planning Staff does not plan the future for SCE. Each officer and manager in the company has the responsibility for developing and implementing short- and long-range plans. The Corporate Planning Staff develops and refines the administrative process for each planning element and then works through that process to develop each element.

Major elements of planning at SCE include organizational plans and program plans. Organizational plans at SCE refer to operations or short-range plans at the organizational level in the company. Each organization in the company prepares a short-range plan of from one to three years. Program plans may be either short- or long-range. Program plans encompass activities that cross organizational boundaries. They provide top management with a tool to focus attention on major activities of SCE.

Elements

The formal planning process at Southern California Edison is very straightforward as far as elements are concerned. The principal elements of the process are the organizational plans, program plans, corporate problems, and corporate assumptions and policies (see Figure 11-1).

Each organization in SCE prepares operational plans for that portion of SCE for which it is responsible. These organizations also forecast significant environmental changes and set forth objectives to respond to that change. Finally, the resources required to carry out their mission are established.

Program plans are used at SCE to focus attention on those major activities that are critical to the overall performance of the company and that need continuing top management direction. The type of major issues that are covered in program plans would be either those that might have an adverse effect on the financial or operating capability of the company or a functional activity that represents a major portion of the total corporate resources.

Corporate problems are problems which the officers and managers of SCE may propose to the Management Committee as being of such serious proportion that special attention must be afforded them. For a matter to be considered a corporate problem, existing management procedures must be inadequate and the problem must be of such significance as to require top management attention. Research and development was initially started in response to a corporate problem and eventually was dealt with as a program plan.

Corporate assumptions are utilized by SCE to provide consistent estimates of the future on which to plan (see Appendix 11A for corporate assumptions). This enables managers in SCE to have a commonly accepted basis for planning and decision making.

Corporate policy at SCE is governed by a very formal process. SCE has had more than thirty published corporate policies with many more in process. Corporate policies at SCE enable top management to control corporate operations.

Time

The formal planning process at SCE has short-range (one- to three-year) operational plans called organizational plans. It also has medium- to long-range plans called program plans. For instance, the plan for electric generating facilities has a horizon of more than 25 years owing to the lead time requirements of the facilities; therefore, it is considered a program plan.

Subject

The subject of the formal planning process at SCE is first production and second financial. The company's unifying purpose for many years has been to meet the expanding product demand. Notwithstanding some outlays for product advertising in the past, marketing has not been a major concern at SCE. With the guaranteed market area possessed by an electric utility, SCE must put emphasis on ensuring reliable service. Much effort must be directed to physical and financial planning for generating plants, transmission lines, and substations. Planning must also be done in other areas such as research and development; but, in the last analysis, much of the research and development affects the facilities of the business.

Characteristics

The planning process at Southern California Edison tends to the formal, complex, rational, flexible, written, strategic, comprehensive, reasonably economical, and effective. It has not been implemented long enough to be operating completely in a steady state. Each new planning cycle reveals innovation in the development of the plans.

Summary

A summary of Steiner's five key dimensions of business planning is outlined in Table 12-2.

One Peter Drucker Concept

In his book *Management Tasks, Responsibilities, and Practices* Peter Drucker states that the idea behind long-range planning is "What *should*

Table 12-2
Summary Analysis of SCE Using Steiner's Criteria

Steiner's Five Dimensions of Business Planning	SCE
Organization	Corporate Planning Staff directs formal planning process; staff essentially a coordinator; substantial planning done at organizational level.
Elements	Major elements include program, resources, and organizational plans; corporate assumptions; corporate policies.
Time	Extremely wide time span—one year to more than 25 years.
Subject	Primarily production; secondarily financial.
Characteristics	Characteristics tend to be formal, complex, written, comprehensive.

our business be?'' He further states that long-range planning should stop managers from assuming that what is a good product, market, service, or technology today will also be good tomorrow.

Peter Drucker has four concepts in the definition of strategic planning: (1) continuous process, (2) entrepreneurial decisions (risk taking for decisions with knowledge of futurity), (3) structured organization (coordinated efforts to carry out the decisions), and (4) systematic feedback (automatic means of measuring actual results against expected performance).

These four concepts in Drucker's definition of strategic planning provide an effective construct for the evaluation of the strategic planning systems of the company. This construct provides a rational framework from which to analyze the various capabilities and capacities of the existing strategic planning system.

Continuous Process

The strategy planning system of SCE is definitely a continuous process. The evolution of the program, resource, and organizational plans continues throughout the year. The Management Committee approves these plans on a staggered basis with approximately one quarter of the plans approved every three months. The strategic planning system provides a continuous evolution of planning throughout this process. Once the plans are approved by the Management Committee, reporting back to the Management Committee is accomplished in accordance with the time schedule set forth in the plan. The corporate problem evolution in the strategic planning system allows major issues of a critical nature to be developed and addressed at any time in the continuous process. The corporate problem-solving process provides the management of SCE with a device for identifying major problems and for allocating the resources necessary to solve them. The strategic planning system allows the Management Committee on a routine basis to examine all the basic decisions made by the various functional organizations of the company and to approve or change them as necessary. Since the strategic planning process is evolutionary throughout the year, SCE provides a specific, continuous process as addressed by Peter Drucker.

Entrepreneurial Decisions

Within the framework of Southern California Edison's strategic planning system, entrepreneurial decisions are routinely made. Drucker's definition of entrepreneurial decisions is risk taking for decisions made with the knowledge of their futurity. One of the basic considerations of a major public utility is that major capital expenditures must be made to bring plant generating capacity on line eight to ten years in the future. For instance, decisions must be made today for increased nuclear generating plants in the late 1980s. These decisions must be made with the best knowledge of the futurity of these decisions. In the past, these decisions were relatively simple to make owing to several environmental factors. First, the lead time on additions to major generating capacity was much less because of the shorter lead times generally available in industry. Also, prior to the building of nuclear plants, the longest lead times were less than half what they are today as a result of the unique requirements for approval and construction of nuclear generating plants. In addition, and possibly most important, over the past two or three decades, electric power usage has been very stable and easily predictable. With the energy crisis in 1973, future usage of electric power became much less stable and much more unpredictable. As a consequence, the strategic planning process of Southern California Edison must be more of an effective participant in the decision-making arena for future generating capacity. Consequently, the SCE system measures up to Drucker's concept of entrepreneurial decisions, but must be more effective in the future.

Structured Organization

Southern California Edison has a very structured organization. Drucker refers to coordinated efforts to carry out decisions reached in the strategic planning process. The Southern California Edison strategic planning system provides a very formal, structured organization and a very finely delineated process by which organizational jurisdiction problems are to be resolved. Not only is the structured organization very clearly set forth, but the jurisdiction statements are approved by the Management Committee after they are developed by each organization unit. Consequently, the efforts of Southern California Edison on a corporate basis are very specifically established in the strategic planning process. By the utilization of the corporate problem-solving process and the jurisdictional statements, responsibility and authority are precisely established. SCE fully measures up to the structured organization concept of Drucker's definition of strategic planning.

Systematic Feedback

Drucker's concept of systematic feedback in the definition of strategic planning involves an automatic means of measuring actual results against expected performance. The system at SCE provides monthly reporting to the Management Committee after the detailed plans are approved. This monthly reporting back to the central decision-making body provides an automatic feedback of results achieved against the projected plan. One of the basic responsibilities of the Management Committee is to review SCE performance against approved plans. This automatic review provides an effective means of systematic feedback of operational results against plans approved by the Management Committee. SCE's strategic planning system complies with Drucker's concept of systematic feedback.

Summary

A summary of Drucker's four concepts of strategic planning is outlined in Table 12-3.

Another Peter Drucker Concept

Another way to compare the strategic planning system of the company is to examine the objectives that have been set for the firm. Objectives are fundamental to the determination of what a firm's business should be. Objectives facilitate the resource allocation process in a firm by establishing the firm's fundamental goals. In *Management, Tasks, Responsibilities and Practices* Peter Drucker provides eight key areas that must be set by top management: (1) marketing, (2) innovation, (3) human organization,

Table 12-3
Summary Analysis of SCE Using Drucker Concepts Criteria

Drucker's Four Concepts in Strategic Planning	SCE
Continuous Process	Program, resource, and organizational plans routinely evolve through the approval process continuously.
Entrepreneurial Decisions	Risk-taking decisions must be made owing to the nature of building power generating plants up to fifteen years in the future.
Structural Organization	Strategic planning is coordinated by the Corporate Planning Staff and accomplished by more than forty organizational units in a closely controlled process.
Systematic Feedback	Feedback is provided monthly to the Management Committee on plans during implementation.

(4) financial resources, (5) physical resources, (6) productivity, (7) social responsibility, and (8) profit requirements.

Marketing objectives are objectives that enable a company to decide who the customer is, who the customer should be, what pricing policy to follow, and what market share to aim for. Innovation objectives are objectives for research, design, or development of new materials, processes, or technology in order to compete effectively in an industry. Human organization objectives are goals for developing workers and managers in areas of recruiting, training, and development. Financial resources objectives are objectives for developing financial resources and measurements to control the resource allocation process. Physical resource objectives are objectives for development of physical resources required by the company. Productivity objectives are objectives for improving the productivity of the company's key resource. Social responsibility objectives are objectives for the social responsibility of the company. Profit requirement is, in a sense, not an objective but a requirement of the company for a certain amount of profit, to be determined by the company, its strategy, its needs, and its risks.

Marketing Objectives

SCE corporate planning system does not treat this area as explicitly as companies with less captive customers. SCE is aware of the marketing aspects of corporate existence and treats them in the corporate planning system, but they have relatively minor roles. (See Appendix 11A, Social Attitudes and Value, as examples of SCE concern.)

Innovation Objectives

The SCE corporate planning system does not set explicit innovation objectives. However, innovation is explicitly discussed and emphasized in the corporate planning system.

Financial Resources

The SCE corporate planning system sets very explicit financial resource objectives in accordance with Drucker's concept. Objectives for developing financial resources and measurements to control the resource allocation process are established in the corporate planning system. (See Figure 11-1 for the Financial Resource Plan.)

Physical Resources

The SCE corporate planning system fully complies with the criteria of Drucker's concept. A substantial part of the corporate planning system is dedicated to developing physical plant. (See Figure 11-1 for an overview of electric facilities resource plans and building and structures program plans. See Appendix 11A for corporate assumptions regarding electric system growth and fuel resources.)

Productivity

The SCE corporate planning system does not establish productivity objectives in accordance with Drucker's concept. However, they do establish explicit plans for each key resource and periodically measure action versus plan. (See Figure 11-1 for an overall view of the corporate planning system.)

Social Responsibility

The SCE corporate planning system does not explicitly establish objectives for corporate responsibility. However, emphasis is put on SCE corporate responsibility in the process. (See Appendix 11A for SCE corporate assumptions on social attitudes and values and human resources.)

Profit Requirement

The SCE corporate planning system sets a profit requirement in accordance with Drucker's concept. SCE establishes financial objectives in its financial program plan with due regard to its capital intensity, cost of capital, and efficient employment of capital. (See Figure 11-1 for an overview of the SCE corporate planning system and Appendix 11A for corporate assumptions on economic business conditions.)

Summary

A summary of Drucker's eight objectives for strategic plans is outlined in Table 12-4.

Table 12-4
Summary Analysis of SCE Using Drucker's Objectives Criteria

Drucker's Eight Objectives for Strategic Plans	SCE
Marketing	No corporate marketing objectives; less important in the utility industry.
Innovation	No corporate innovation objectives; however, company relies on new nuclear technology.
Human Organization	No corporate human organization objectives; however, detailed corporate assumptions provide human basis for organizational planning.
Financial Resources	Explicit financial resource objectives are established; process is central for a capital-intensive utility.
Physical Resources	Explicit physical resource objectives are established; forms the nucleus of the total corporate planning system.
Productivity	No corporate productivity objectives; key resources are subject to extensive planning and measurement.
Social Responsibilities	No corporate social responsibility objectives; however, detailed corporate assumptions provide social responsibilities for organizational planning.
Profit	Corporate profit requirements are established; financial program plans cover in detail.

Part III
Conclusion

13 Research Findings and Conclusions

Previous chapters have included a detailed description of the concept of strategic long-range planning, the environment of the energy industry, a description of the strategic planning system of a major United States company, and an analysis of the strategic planning system of the company.

Conclusions of strategic planning research will be presented in this chapter. Each subhypothesis will be discussed, and then the basic hypothesis of the research will be discussed. Next, the implications of the research for general management will be presented, followed by a concluding summary.

Subhypotheses

Subhypothesis One

The first subhypothesis posits that the farther the company operates from the production sector of the industry, the longer the planning horizon will be of a corporation operating in the uncertain and rapidly changing environment of the energy industry. This is substantiated as follows:

	Caltex	Hudson	SCE
Planning time horizon	5 years	8 to 10 years	25 years

The basic planning time horizons of the Caltex strategic planning system are as follows: An initial five-year planning cycle, next a three-year planning cycle, and finally a one-year expense budget and a three-year investment budget. Each year, at the initiation of the planning cycle, projections are made for five years. Five-year projections include forecasts for consumption, sales, and market share for crude oil and crude oil products. Other five-year forecasts include supply assumptions, crude oil profits and availability, refinery and pipeline capacities, refinery requirements and

---

For a further discussion of this subject, the interested reader should examine the dissertation "Strategic Planning in a Rapidly Changing Environment: Energy Companies and the Energy Industry," (the University of Michigan, Ann Arbor, 1975). In it, the planning systems of CALTEX Petroleum Corporation, Hudson Oil Co., Inc., and SCE were studied to determine the impact of planning on the strategic decisions of each firm.

runs, and tanker requirements. These basic forecasts for sales and supply requirements form the basis for the strategic planning system at Caltex.

Based on the initial five-year projections, the second phase, or three-year program, is established in the Caltex strategic planning system. Trading company forecasts for sales of crude oil, refined products and lubricating oils and grease are made for a three-year period. Then pricing assumptions for crude oil, refined products, and tanker rates are forecast for three years.

At this point, the strategic planning system consolidates the information desired thus far into a financial plan which includes expense budgets and investment budgets. The board of directors then approves a one-year expense budget and a three-year investment budget. The basic planning time horizon of the Caltex strategic planning system is five years and provides an approved three-year investment budget and one-year expense budget.

The basic planning horizons at Hudson Oil Company, Inc., are difficult to detect since there is no formal strategic planning system. Strategic planning at Hudson is primarily done by the president. Planning in the past has had to address the questions of new station location. However, the basic environment Hudson operates in changed drastically in the mid-1970s. Strategic issues now include assured sources of supply for Hudson stations.

The basic planning horizon at Hudson has been relatively short, but is now lengthening to eight to ten years for refinery planning. Strategic planning, even though done by one or two individuals, must have sufficient planning horizons.

The basic planning cycle at SCE contains the following horizons:

1. A 25-year planning cycle in generating plant
2. A 5-year planning cycle in organization plans
3. A 5-year planning cycle in program plans
4. A 1-year cycle for the approved portion of the annual plans

The SCE strategic planning system calls for an annual updating of all plans. The cycle is established on a quarterly basis so that one-fourth of all company plans come up for quarterly approval. Plans are processed through the system and then brought for approval before the Management Committee. Once the plans are approved, the manager of the organization or unit involved implements the approved plan.

The longest planning cycle is that for the plant required for generation capacity. In the past, the long-term demand for electricity has been relatively easy to forecast. A model has been used to predict customer demand for kilowatt consumption. Then SCE used another model to optimize the location and establishment of facilities. The basic forecasting was accomplished using demographic variables. For SCE to be able to forecast effectively for

25 years is justification for the basic hypothesis of this study. There is no way in the uncertainty of the production sector that a corporation could forecast 25 years with any semblance of accuracy.

The basic five-year cycle used in the program and organizational plans provide the one-year plan that is approved by the Management Committee and implemented by SCE managers.

The length of the planning time horizon is affected by the level of uncertainty extant in the environments of the different companies in the energy industry. Caltex operates closest to the production (most uncertain) sector in the continuum of the energy industry. SCE operates the furthest from the production sector. The strategic planning practices of these companies reflect the influences of those varying levels of uncertainty.

Subhypothesis Two

The second hypothesis posits that the farther the company operates from the production sector of the industry, the more corporate planning models will be used. Corporate planning models are defined as computer models which use simulation techniques. This is substantiated as follows:

	Caltex	*Hudson*	*SCE*
Uses corporate planning models	No	No	Yes

Caltex does not use corporate planning models in its strategic planning process. As Caltex develops the forecasted usage of energy and ultimately petroleum products in the countries in which it operates, the company uses various methods of analysis to try to determine the forecast usage of those countries. However, in the entire planning process, Caltex does not utilize any corporate models.

Hudson Oil does not use a corporate planning model. Strategic planning at Hudson is accomplished by the president or executive vice president. Since Hudson does not have a formal planning system, it has little need for a corporate planning model.

SCE utilizes a corporate planning model in its strategic planning process. The model includes 61 data inputs utilized in four separate models. These models include a revenue model, an operating-cost model, a construction model, and a finance model. Projections of up to fifteen years are possible. The four models are linked to one another so that the effects of a change in plans in one model would be reflected in all the others. All four models are then consolidated into a fifth model. Then the effect on SCE strategy can be examined.

The model is primarily a financial one that allows SCE to use varying levels of sales and expenditures and to predict various financial figures such as earnings per share, net income, and other important financial figures. These forecasts are used in the formal planning process to ask "what if" questions such as, If the earnings per share in 1979 is forecast to drop by 20 percent, what would happen if SCE cut planned expenditures by 10 percent? The model has been used for several years, but it has not been completely accepted by top management. They view it with some skepticism but essentially as a part of the overall planning system to point management to better questions, better answers, and ultimately more effective decision making.

The use of corporate planning models also reflects on the amount of uncertainty extant in the environment. Caltex would have little use for a model such as the one SCE uses, because of rapid changes in the environment. The long-term trends of SCE's environment are extremely helpful to a corporate planning model.

Subhypothesis Three

The third subhypothesis posits that the stretegic planning system of a corporation operating in the uncertain and rapidly changing environment of the energy industry will be less centralized as the company operates farther from the production sector. This is substantiated as follows:

	Caltex	*Hudson*	*SCE*
Degree of planning centralization	High	Highest	Lower

The strategic planning process at Caltex is very centralized. Planning is done in the Planning and Economics Department. When projections are made for consumption, sales, and market position for crude oil and crude oil products, the Planning and Economics Department does substantial analytical work on these forecasts. When quality forecasts and general policy assumptions are made, the Planning and Economics Department has a substantial input. When supply requirements and assumptions are established, the Planning and Economics Department plays a substantial role.

The strategic planning process at Hudson is highly centralized. Strategic planning is accomplished by the president or the executive vice president. The centralization of strategic planning authority could hardly be improved.

The strategic planning process at SCE is not highly centralized. Although the Corporate Planning Staff was established to direct functionally the strategic planning process, it acts primarily as a coordinator and an integrator.

The Corporate Planning Staff does not plan the future of SCE. That is the responsibility of each officer and manager in the company. Each officer and manager is responsible for developing and implementing both short- and long-range plans.

Personnel preparing corporate plans for SCE are highly decentralized. More than forty organizational plans and more than ten program plans are developed by different people and organizations in the company. They are prepared by the personnel that are responsible for the unit or program for which the plan is created and who must then implement the plan. The Corporate Planning Staff assists the planning being accomplished throughout the company by providing assistance and in-depth comments when requested.

Ultimately, when the plans are presented to the Management Committee for approval, the Corporate Planning Staff acts as a staff to the committee. Although the Corporate Planning Staff had little input into the plans initially, as the process moves through a complete cycle, it provides continuity to the entire strategic planning process at SCE.

Subhypothesis Four

The fourth subhypothesis is that the strategic planning system of a corporation operating in the uncertain and rapidly changing environment of the energy industry will be on a lower organizational level as the company operates farther from the production sector. This is substantiated as follows:

	Caltex	*Hudson*	*SCE*
Organizational level of planning	Reports to president	President and executive vice president	Throughout organization

The strategic planning process at Caltex is on a high organizational level. The manager of the Planning and Economics Department reports directly to the president.

Strategic planning at Hudson could not be accomplished at a higher level, for it is done by the president and the executive vice president.

The strategic planning process at SCE is on a lower organizational level. The more than forty organizational plans and ten program plans are a substantial amount of the strategic planning process. They are prepared throughout the organization.

Even the coordination of the SCE strategic planning process is on a lower level than the actual planning of the other two companies. The manager of corporate planning has been two to three management levels lower during the past seven years.

Subhypothesis Five

The fifth subhypothesis states that the strategic planning system of a corporation operating in the uncertain and rapidly changing environment of the energy industry will utilize more sophisticated forecasting techniques as the company operates farther from the production sector. This subhypothesis is substantiated as follows:

	Caltex	*Hudson*	*SCE*
Uses sophisticated forecasting techniques	No	No	Yes

In the strategic planning process at Caltex, sophisticated forecasting techniques are not used. When the Planning and Economic Department is establishing energy-use forecasts for the countries in which Caltex operates, it uses correlation and regression computer programs. However, it uses no techniques more sophisticated than that.

However, this information should not be too startling. Even though sophisticated forecasting techniques might have an overall positive effect on decision making at Caltex, the company may be in too uncertain an environment to utilize available techniques effectively. Although the information of the research does not support the hypothesis as stated, it provides support to the hypothesis that companies operating in a more certain environment can use more sophisticated forecasting techniques than companies operating in a more uncertain environment.

Hudson Oil Company, Inc., does not use sophisticated forecasting techniques in its strategic planning. Any forecasting that might be accomplished is the result of the reasoned estimates of two persons.

SCE uses several sophisticated forecasting models in its strategic planning process. First, the financial corporate planning model provides top management with decision-making flexibility by providing answers to "what if" questions in the financial portion of the company. Second, a model is used in systems planning to forecast the required load for SCE. The model utilizes demographic variables to predict customer demand for the consumption of kilowatthours up to 20 years in the future. Demand is the total amount of system capacity, and consumption is the amount of fuel required. Third, a model is used to determine when and where facilities should be established once customer demand has been forecasted.

Summary

Table 13-1 summarizes the three planning systems and the five subhypotheses.

Basic Hypothesis

The basic hypothesis tested is that the strategic planning system of a corporation operating in the uncertain and rapidly changing environment of the energy industry will be more formal (an identified part of the management structure and systems) and more effective (an identified influence upon general management decisions) as the company operates farther from the production (the most uncertain) sector of the industry.

The definition used for *formal* in the context of strategic planning is that the strategic planning system has been an identified part of the management structure and systems. Caltex and SCE both have formal strategic planning systems. Hudson Oil Company, Inc., does not have a strategic planning system that is an identified part of the management structure and systems. Strategic planning at Hudson is accomplished informally by the two top executives.

Hudson does not have a strategic planning system in the usual sense.

Table 13-1
Strategic Planning Subhypothesis Summary

	Caltex	Hudson	SCE
Planning time horizon	5 years	8 to 10 years	25 years
Uses corporate planning models	No	No	Yes
Degree of planning centralization	High	Highest	Lower
Organizational level of planning	Reports to president	President and executive vice-president	Throughout the organization
Uses sophisticated forecasting techniques	No	No	Yes

However, if a distinction can be made between an implicit strategic planning system and an explicit strategic planning system, Hudson has an implicit strategic planning system. Strategic decisions are made by the president and the executive vice president routinely. However, an explicit, well-defined strategic planning system does not exist in Hudson Oil Company. The strategic decisions made by top management reflect the implicit structure that is available.

The Caltex system is formal. It is an identified part of the management structure and systems. However, it deals primarily with economic uncertainty in the environment. The scope and therefore the overall impact of the system are less than they would be if they covered more than economic uncertainty.

The Caltex strategic planning system is an important part of the management structure and systems of the corporation. As the different consumption and sales forecasts are being developed, and later when supply requirements are being developed prior to the eventual establishment of a one-year expense budget and a three-year investment budget, the Caltex planning system is an integral part of the management structure.

However, the SCE strategic planning system is a more formal system. The SCE system can also easily be identified as a part of the management structure and systems. The Management Committee at SCE meets weekly to review organization and program plans. The Executive Committee at Caltex meets an average of once a month to review portions of the Caltex system. Follow-ups to the SCE system are accomplished within the system and reported back to the Management Committee. Follow-ups at Caltex are the responsibility of accounting personnel at headquarters and may not be reported back to the Executive Committee. Corporate problems at SCE may be brought to the attention of the Management Committee by a formally established procedure. Corporate problems at Caltex may not be brought to the attention of the Executive Committee through the strategic planning system. The financial plans at SCE are submitted and approved via the strategic planning process, while at Caltex the Planning and Economics Department provides input to financial planning for the three-year portion of the planning process. Corporate assumptions at SCE are formally updated semiannually, while various assumptions at Caltex are an integral part of the process. Corporate policies are written explicitly at SCE to provide corporate guidance, while there is no such explicit procedure in the Caltex strategic planning system. Detailed organizational and program plans are developed within the SCE strategic planning process, while at Caltex the overall one-year expense budget and three-year investment budget are developed.

The organizational development of the Corporate Planning Committee substantiates the more formal strategic planning process at SCE as much as any other single factor. The committee originally reported to the vice president in charge of engineering, finance, and rates through the manager of systems development. Then the name was changed to the Management Committee, while still retaining corporate planning responsibility. The membership was changed to include the president, two senior vice presidents, and four vice presidents. The committee was reconstituted again to include the chairman of the board, the president, and two executive vice presidents. The Management Committee, headed by the chairman of the board, now meets weekly to make decisions in the framework of the SCE strategic planning system.

The definition used for *effective* with reference to strategic planning in this study is that the strategic planning system has been an identified influence upon general management decisions. Caltex and SCE both have effective strategic planning systems. Hudson Oil Company, Inc., does not have a strategic planning system that is an identified influence on general management decisions.

General management decisions at Caltex are made by the Executive Committee. The strategic planning process at Caltex provides various decision points as the system moves toward final approval of the one-year expense budget and three-year investment budget. These decision points include (1) initially approving the strategic planning schedule for the year, (2) reviewing greenbook forecasts, (3) reviewing redbook assumptions, (4) reviewing preliminary and final investment programs, and (5) reviewing preliminary and final financial programs culminating in the final budget approvals. Throughout this period, the strategic planning system has an identified influence on general management decisions at Caltex.

However, the scope of this influence is limited. Of the various types of uncertainty extant in the Caltex environment, the Caltex strategic planning system only provides for economic uncertainty. The other four types of uncertainty are not addressed or handled by the Caltex strategic planning process.

On the other hand, the strategic planning process at SCE addresses and handles all types of uncertainty identified in this study. Not only is the economic uncertainty extant in the environment addressed and handled by the SCE strategic planning process, but the political, ecological, technological, and social uncertainty is also. The scope and therefore the influence on general management decision are much broader in the SCE system than in the Caltex system.

The Management Committee at SCE meets weekly on subjects in the strategic planning system, while the Caltex Executive Committee meets much less frequently on subjects in the Caltex strategic planning system.

Corporate problems can be initiated in the SCE strategic planning system and will impact the general management decisions of the firm. Corporate problems at Caltex will be brought to the attention of top management outside the strategic planning system.

As shown above, the strategic planning system of SCE is more formal and more effective than those of Caltex or Hudson. SCE is the company located the farthest from the production sector of the industry.

One annual occurrence at SCE lends credence to the substance of the basic hypothesis. Of all the more than fifty organizational and program plans that must be written each year, the most trouble by far is caused by the organizational element called fuel supply, the closest organization in SCE to the production sector of the energy industry.

Implications for General Management

Strategic planning has been described earlier as being concerned with definition of organizational goals. Furthermore, strategic planning is concerned with the design of functional policies and plans and the organizational structure and systems to achieve organizational objectives. All this is accomplished in response to an analysis of the environmental characteristics and trends, organizational resources and skills, and managerial motives and values.

The major implication for general management that is raised is the significant importance and rate of change of the environmental variable. Of the three companies covered in the analysis of their strategic planning systems, the most far-reaching system, the most formal system, and the most effective system were extant where there is the least environmental tumult. General management must be made aware that strategic planning solely for the sake of having strategic planning is not efficacious. Strategic planning must be given sufficient top management attention and resources to ensure that a company, in fact, does accomplish effective long-range planning when its environment is subject to rapid change.

It is relatively easy for a major public utility to have a formal, long-range planning system to plan twenty to twenty-five years ahead, owing to the demands of its industry. However, it is unusual to find a central corporate planning staff in a major public utility.

Although the public utilities are operating in a less rapidly changing environment than many other companies in the energy industry, the rate of environmental change is increasing. As a consequence, the top management of public utilities should consider giving the strategic planning function more attention and resources and develop formal long-range planning systems that are more than just a forecast of future construction requirements.

If management does not devote sufficient effort to strategic planning, certain circumstances in the future will affect the company in ways they would not have originally chosen. However, particularly in the rapidly changing environment of the energy industries, this is even more critical. The energy environment is rapidly increasing in uncertainty. Relatively placid scenarios taken for granted five years ago are seething with vast implications for top management.

When strategic plans are established, importance must be given to the skills and resources of the organization and the changes in it. It is most difficult to establish an effective strategic planning system in an extremely rapidly changing environment. It is much simpler to say that the environment is changing so quickly that top management cannot take the time required to devote to a corporate planning effort. However, for the very reason that the environment does change rapidly, top management must find the requisite time for strategic planning.

As projects are becoming more costly each year, as paybacks are lengthening each year, as management has to be aware of a larger array of technical information, the more the strategic decision process of the firm must be influenced by its strategic planning process. This may not happen where it is most imperative because of the difficulty of the task. Therefore, top management must make it occur.

This is not to say that companies in the sector of the environment that shows the most rapid change will not have strategic planning systems. Most large companies today have some sort of strategic planning system. However, the company in a rapidly changing environment that takes the time and effort to have both the form and the substance of an effective strategic planning program should be paid back many fold in the last analysis.

The implication for general managers is rather challenging. To see very effective and detailed corporate planning systems in operation in very stable environments is to question the function or role they are playing.

Is the corporate planning process being effectively utilized in the overall management of the firm? Are the strategic decisions in the firm or those concerned with the long-term development of the firm actually made within the corporate planning process? Or does management allow the very detailed corporate planning process to ponder only those problems of the enterprise with no strategic significance?

Implications for Managers of Corporate Planning Staffs

A very practical yet frustrating implication comes from this research. The possibility presents itself very strongly that the easiest planning challenges and the most detailed plans may have the least impact on the strategic future of the organization. The part of the enterprise that has a difficult time planning may be grappling with the major strategic issues facing the company.

The manager of a corporate planning staff must be more concerned with the substance of plans and the potential strategic questions involved than with the number of plans submitted on time and the routine follow-ups that must be made.

When corporate planning systems are initially established in a company, it may be tempting to start in areas easy to plan owing to a stable environment. However, much effort should be allocated to those parts of the company where planning not only will be the most difficult because of the rapidly changing environment but also will produce the best long-run contributions of strategic importance to the firm.

Conclusion

The concept of strategic planning is a powerful one. However, to achieve an effective strategic planning system, an organization must expend a great deal of effort. The nature of strategic planning makes the process difficult. The firm must examine its external and internal environment and determine what type of a business it wants to be in the future. The requirement to analyze the external environment for a United States firm has never been more important to its long-term well being, and the external environmental analysis has never been more difficult. These trends are not expected to change. Aggressive firms must learn to deal with and change their operating environment in order to achieve their overall objectives.

To have an effective strategic planning system, an organization must build on the capabilities available. The organization must know what its capabilities are and then develop its strategy based upon them. A firm must not ignore what is happening in its market place; it must use financial analysis to understand it. Organizations must approach the future with more flexibility than they have in the past. What are the implications of future changes? What happens if a certain market shifts or a new trend becomes the future way of doing business? Objectives should be set for the organization as a whole and for its important parts. These objectives provide a consistency of action and purpose for managers throughout the organization. Quantify these objectives as much as possible, and get agreement from managers throughout the organization.

Critically evaluate alternative plans that are available to the organization. Make decisions based upon the best financial analysis available. Be sure that plans are understood by critical managers and that the plans are internally consistent. Strategic planning provides the means for the organization as a whole to be working for consistent objectives. The overall strategy of the organization should have appeal. Managers and personnel should be able to identify with the strategy and work for its success.

Successful plans must be implemented by the line portion of the organization. Make sure that the systems which are integrally involved in the overall management of the organization (such as control, information, compensation, and planning) are all internally consistent and support the corporate strategy of the organization.

Finally, strategic planning is a general management function. Top management cannot delegate the responsibility for strategic planning. Top management must actively support and be involved with the strategic planning system in any organization, or else it will not be as effective as it could be. Strategic planning provides a sound concept for improving the management of organizations. It is up to managers to make it work.

Bibliography

Books and Reports

Ackoff, Russell L. *A Concept of Corporate Planning*. New York: Wiley-Interscience, 1970.

Adelman, M.A. *The World Petroleum Market*. Baltimore, Md.: The Johns Hopkins University Press, 1972.

Adelman, M.A.; Bradley, Paul G.; and Norman, Charles A. *Alaskan Oil: Costs and Supply*. New York: Praeger Publishers, 1971.

Aguilar, Francis J.; Howell, Robert A.; and Vancil, Richard R. *Formal Planning Systems—1970*. Cambridge, Mass.: Harvard Business School, 1970.

Allvine, Fred C., and Patterson, James M. *Competition Ltd.: The Marketing of Gasoline*. Bloomington, Ind.: Indiana University Press, 1972.

Andrews, Kenneth R. *The Concept of Corporate Strategy*. Homewood, Ill.: Dow Jones-Irvin, Inc., 1971.

Anthony, Robert N. *Planning and Control Systems: A Framework for Analysis*. Cambridge, Mass.: Harvard Business School, 1965.

Anyon, G. Jay. *Entrepreneurial Dimensions of Management*. Wynnewood, Pa.: Livingston, 1973.

Argenti, John. *Corporate Planning: A Practical Guide*. London, England: George Allen and Unwin, Ltd., 1968.

Barnard, Chester I. *The Functions of the Executive*. Cambridge, Mass.: Harvard University Press, 1954.

Bauer, Raymond A., and Gergen, Kenneth J., eds. *The Study of Policy Formation*. New York: The Free Press, 1968.

Bonge, John W., and Coleman, Bruce P. *Concepts for Corporate Strategy*. New York: The Macmillan Company, 1972.

Boulden, James B. *Computer-Assisted Planning Systems*. New York: McGraw-Hill Book Company, 1976.

Bower, Joseph L. *Managing the Resource Allocation Process*. Cambridge, Mass.: The Harvard Business School, 1970.

Bower, Marvin. *The Will to Manage*. New York: McGraw-Hill Book Company, 1966.

Branch, Melville C. *The Corporate Planning Process*. New York: McGraw-Hill Book Company, 1966.

Bright, James R., ed. *Technological Forecasting for Industry and Government*. Englewood Cliffs, N.J.: Prentice-Hall, Inc., 1968.

Brown, James K., and O'Connor, Rochelle. *Planning and the Corporate Planning Director*. New York: The Conference Board, Inc., 1974.

Burght, James R., and Schoeman, Milton. *A Guide to Practical Technological Forecasting*. Englewood Cliffs, N.J.: Prentice-Hall, Inc., 1973.

Burrows, James C., and Domencich, Thomas A. *An Analysis of the United States Oil Import Quota*. Lexington, Mass.: D.C. Heath and Co.

Caves, Richard. *American Industry: Structure, Conduct, Performance*. 3d ed. Englewood Cliffs, N.J.: Prentice-Hall, Inc., 1972.

Champernowne, P.G. *Uncertainty and Estimation in Economics*. Edinburgh: Oliver & Boyd, 1969.

Chandler, Alfred D., Jr. *Strategy and Structure: Chapters on the History of the American Industrial Enterprise*. Cambridge, Mass.: The M.I.T. Press, 1962.

Collier, James R. *Effective Long-Range Business Planning*. Englewood Cliffs, N.J.: Prentice-Hall, Inc., 1968.

Corey, E. Raymond, and Star, Steven H. *Organization Strategy: A Marketing Approach*. Cambridge, Mass.: Harvard Business School, 1971.

Davies, Duncan, and McCarthy, Collum. *Introduction to Technological Economics*. London: John Wiley & Sons, 1967.

Drucker, Peter F. *Management Tasks—Responsibilities—Practices*. New York: Harper and Row, Publishers, 1973.

Egerton, Henry C., and Brown, James K. *Planning and the Chief Executive*. New York: The Conference Board, Inc., 1972.

Energy Policy of the Ford Foundation. *Exploring Energy Choices*. Washington, D.C., 1971.

Engler, Robert. *The Politics of Oil*. New York: The MacMillan Company, 1961.

Ewing, David W. *Long Range Planning for Management*. New York: Harper and Brothers, 1958.

Fox, Anthony Francis. *The World of Oil*. New York: The MacMillan Company, 1964.

Hainer, Raymond M.; Kingsbury, Shormon; and Gleicher, David B., eds. *Uncertainty in Research, Management, and New Product Development*. New York: Reinhold Publishing Corporation, 1967.

Harrison, E. Frank. *The Managerial Decision-Making Process*. Boston: Houghton Mifflin, 1975.

Harrison, E. Frank. *Management and Organization*. Boston: Houghton Mifflin, 1978.

Henry, Harold W. *Long-Range Planning Practices in 45 Industrial Companies*. Englewood Cliffs, N.J.: Prentice-Hall, Inc., 1967.

Hosmer, Larce T.; Cooper, Arnold C.; and Vesper, Karl H. *The Entrepreneurial Function*. Englewood Cliffs, N.J.: Prentice-Hall, Inc., 1977.

Kahn, Herman, and Wiener, Anthony J. *The Year 2000*. New York: The MacMillan Company, 1967.

Katz, Robert L. *Cases and Concepts in Corporate Strategy.* Englewood Cliffs, N.J.: Prentice-Hall, Inc., 1970.

Landsberg, H.S., and Schurr, S.H. *Energy in the United States.* New York: Random House, 1968.

Le Breton, Preston P., and Henning, Dale A. *Planning Theory.* Englewood Cliffs, N.J.: Prentice-Hall, Inc., 1961.

Mack, Ruth P. *Planning on Uncertainty.* New York: Wiley-Interscience, 1971.

McLean, John G., and Haigh, Robert William. *The Growth of Integrated Oil Companies.* Boston: Division of Research, Graduate School of Business Administration, Harvard University, 1954.

McCarthy, Daniel J.; Minichiello, Robert J.; and Curran, Joseph R. *Business Policy and Strategy.* Homewood, Ill.: Richard D. Irwin, Inc., 1975.

Mockler, Robert J., ed. *Readings in Business Planning and Policy Formulation.* New York: Appleton-Century Crofts, 1972.

National Petroleum Council. *U.S. Energy Outlook.* Vols. 1 and 2. Washington, D.C., 1971.

O'Connor, Rochelle. *Corporate Guide to Long-Range Planning.* New York: The Conference Board, Inc., 1976.

Quade, E.S., and Boucher, W.I. *Systems Analysis and Policy Planning Applications in Defense.* New York: American Elsevier Publishing Company, Inc., 1968.

Rifai, Taki. *The Pricing of Crude Oil.* New York: Praeger Publishers, Inc., 1974.

Rogers, David C.D. *Corporate Strategy and Long Range Planning.* Ann Arbor, Mich.: The Landis Press, 1973.

Rogers, David C.D. *The Manager's Guide to Budgeting, Inventory Analysis and Management Control Systems.* Ann Arbor, Mich.: The Landis Press, 1973.

Rogers, David C.D. *Business Policy and Planning.* Englewood Cliffs, N.J.: Prentice-Hall, Inc., 1977.

Rudwick, Bernard H. *Systems Analysis for Effective Planning.* New York: John Wiley and Sons, Inc., 1969.

Schurr, Sam H., and Netschert, Bruce C. *Energy in the American Economy, 1950-1975.* Baltimore, Md.: The Johns Hopkins Press, 1960.

Schwendiman, John Snow. *Strategic Long-Range Planning for the Multi-National Corporation.* New York: Praeger Publishers, Inc., 1973.

Scott, Brian W. *Long Range Planning in American Industry.* New York: American Management Association, Inc., 1965.

Selznick, Philip. *Leadership in Administration.* New York: Harper & Row, 1957.

Spence, Hartzell. *Portrait in Oil.* New York: McGraw-Hill Book Company, Inc., 1962.

Steiner, George A., ed. *Managerial Long-Range Planning.* New York: McGraw-Hill Book Company, Inc., 1963.

Steiner, George A. *Top Management Planning.* New York: The MacMillan Company, 1969.

Steiner, George A., and Miner, John B. *Management Policy and Strategy.* New York: Macmillan Publishing Co., Inc., 1977.

Stoner, James A.F. *Management.* Englewood Cliffs, N.J.: Prentice-Hall, Inc., 1978.

Vancil, Richard F.; Aguilar, Francis J.; Howell, Robert A.; and McFarlan, F. Warren. *Formal Planning Systems—1969.* Cambridge, Mass.: Harvard Business School, 1969.

Warren, E. Kirby. *Long-Range Planning: The Executive Viewpoint.* Englewood Cliffs, N.J.: Prentice-Hall, Inc., 1966.

Williamson, Harold F.; Andreano, Ralph L.; Baum, Arnold R.; and Klose, Gilbert C. *The American Petroleum Industry.* Evanston, Ill.: Northwestern University Press, 1963.

Articles

Anshen, Melvin, and Guth, William D. "Strategies for Research in Policy Formulation." *Journal of Business,* October 1973.

Ansoff, H. Igor. "The Concept of Strategic Management." *Journal of Business Policy*, Summer 1972.

Cammillus, J.C. "Evaluating the Benefits of Formal Planning Systems." *Long Range Planning*, June 1975.

Cohen, Kelman J., and Cyert, Richard M. "Strategy: Formulation, Implementation, and Monitoring." *The Journal of Business*, pp. 349-67.

Gonzales, Richard J. "Interfuel Competition for Future Energy Markets." *Journal of the Institute of Petroleum* 54 (July 1968): 177-81.

Hall, William K. "Strategic Planning Models—Are Top Managers Really Finding Them Useful?" *Journal of Business Policy*, Fall 1972.

Khandwalla, Pradip N. "Environment and Its Impact on the Organization." *International Studies of Management and Organization,* Fall 1972, pp. 297-313.

Linneman, Robert E., and Kennell, John D. "Shirt-Sleeve Approach to Long Range Plans." *Harvard Business Review*, March-April 1977, pp. 141-50.

Miller, O. "Towards a Contingency Theory of Strategy Formulation." *Academy of Management Proceedings*, August 1975.

159

Mintzberg, Henry. "Strategy-Making in Three Modes." *California Management Review*, Winter 1973, pp. 44-53.

Mockler, Robert J. "Theory and Practice of Planning." *Harvard Business Review*, March-April 1970, pp. 148-59.

Mones, Rene. "The Quality and Pricing of Crude Oil, the American Experience." *Journal of International Economics*, March 1964.

Ringbakk, K.A. "New Concepts for Strategic Planning." *Planning Review*, March 1975.

Taylor, Ronald N. "Psychological Aspects of Planning." *Long Range Planning*, April 1976.

Thune, Stanley S., and House, Robert J. "Where Long-Range Planning Pays Off." *Business Horizons*, August 1970, pp. 85-87.

Vancil, Richard F., and Lorange, Peter. "Strategic Planning in Diversified Companies." *Harvard Business Review*, January-February 1975, pp. 81-90.

Index

Index

164

Information system, 58
Innovation objectives, 135, 136, 138
Integration, 16, 42, 63

Key result areas, 107

Management committee, 99-101, 117
Manager of corporate planning, 99
Marketing objectives, 135, 136, 138
Marketing sector, 86, 92-96
Money market rates, 82
Motivation, 59

Natural gas consumption, 72, 74
Natural gas imports, 74
Natural gas reserves, 75, 78
North Sea, 78
North Slope, 78
Nuclear power plant capacity, 77

Objectives, 35, 135; financial resources,
  136, 138; innovation, 135, 136, 138;
  marketing, 136, 138; physical
  resources, 137, 138; productivity,
  137, 138; profit requirement, 137,
  138; social responsibility, 137, 138
Oil consumption, 72
Oil wells, 72, 73
OPEC, 82
Operational management, 4
Organization, 130, 132
Organizational jurisdiction, 108
Organizational level of planning, 145,
  147
Organizational planning process, 113
Organizational structure, 54, 128
Organizational systems, 128
Organization plan, 50, 111-112
Organizing, 9, 55
Overview, 7

Performance standards, 64
Personal strategy, 41
Personal values, 17, 127
Pervading, concept of, 63
Physical resource objectives, 137, 138
Planning basis, 27

Planning cycle, 142
Planning horizons, 142, 147
Plans, 47
Policies, 47
Policy formulation, 48
Political environment, 3, 20, 22, 23, 36
Political trends, 28, 36, 102, 120
Political uncertainty, 79, 86, 87, 89,
  149
Population, 83
Problem identification, 116
Producing deep well, 78
Production sector, 76, 92-96
Productivity objectives, 137, 138
Profitless growth, 43
Profit requirement objectives, 137, 138
Program plan, 51, 105, 131
Program planning process, 107

Reconciliation, 127
Refineries, 84; capacity, 84; input, 85
Reorganization process, 111
Resource allocation, 40
Resource analysis, 15
Resources, 15, 126
Responsibility, for corporate objec-
  tives, 36; strategic planning, 9

Service stations, 88; total, 88; total retail sales, 88
Short term plan, 50
Social attitudes, and values, 30, 102,
  119
Social environment, 3, 20, 22
Social responsibility objectives, 137,
  138
Social trends, 22
Social uncertainty, 76, 82, 86, 88, 90,
  96, 149
Society's interests, 127
Southern California Edison Company,
  97, 125, 141-150; corporate assumptions, 101, 119; corporate planning
  committee, 99; corporate planning
  manual, 97; corporate planning process, 97; corporate planning staff
  100; corporate policy, 102; cor-

About the Author

James B. Whittaker is a member of the faculty of the Georgetown University School of Business Administration. He received the B.S. degree from the University of Kansas and M.B.A. and Ph.D. degrees from the University of Michigan. Dr. Whittaker teaches in the areas of policy and control. He has taught on the faculty of George Washington University, The University of Michigan and the Catholic University of America.

Dr. Whittaker is also on the faculty of the Management Education Department of the Graduate School of Business Administration of The University of Michigan in Ann Arbor, Michigan. At Michigan he has developed and taught a number of management seminars.